St John Henry Newman

Hermann Geissler, FSO

St John Henry Newman: A New Doctor of the Church

IGNATIUS PRESS SAN FRANCISCO

All quotations from papal and council documents are from the Vatican website.

Cover image: *John Henry Newman* by Herbert Rose Barraud
Public domain, via Wikimedia Commons
Half title page: *John Henry Newman* by George Richmond, 1844
Mary Evans Picture Library

This edition published in 2026 by Ignatius Press, San Francisco
Print ISBN 978-1-62164-940-3
eBook ISBN 978-1-64229-425-5
Library of Congress Control Number 2026933963
Printed in the United States of America ♾

Contents

About the Author

Father Hermann Geissler, FSO, born on 12 June 1965 in Hall in Tirol (Austria), studied at the Benedict XVI Philosophical-Theological University in Heiligenkreuz/Vienna and earned a doctorate in theology from the Pontifical Lateran University in Rome with a thesis on "Conscience and Truth in the Writings of Cardinal John Henry Newman". A member since 1988 of the Spiritual Family The Work, he was ordained a priest in 1991. From 1993 to 2019 he worked at the Congregation for the Doctrine of the Faith; in 2009 Benedict XVI appointed him head of the doctrinal section. He has published numerous articles on the life, spirituality, and theology of John Henry Newman, on Mother Julia Verhaeghe, the founder of the Spiritual Family The Work, and on current topics of ecclesial life. He is the director of the International Centre of Newman Friends in Rome (*www.newmanfriendsinternational.org*), a formator in the Priests' Community of The Work, and a professor of theology at various theological institutions in Italy and Austria.

Introduction

"The characteristic of the great Doctor of the Church, it seems to me, is that he teaches not only through his thought and speech but also by his life, because within him, thought and life are interpenetrated and defined. If this is so, then Newman belongs to the great teachers of the Church, because he both touches our hearts and enlightens our thinking."[1] With these words Cardinal Joseph Ratzinger expressed 35 years ago what Pope Leo XIV officially declared on 1 November 2025: St John Henry Newman is to be numbered among the Doctors of the Church.

During his long life (1801–1890) Newman was not always fully understood. As an Anglican he had to endure a great deal of criticism, accusation, and mistrust because he strove to renew the Church of England in the spirit of the Church Fathers, and in so doing he drew ever closer to Catholicism. After his conversion he was repeatedly exposed to misunderstanding and slander, and for some years was even suspected of heresy, because he openly reflected on new questions and did not use the language of classical theology. He himself maintained that he was not a theologian in the strict sense, and in fact he did not think according to scholastic categories or concern himself with the ideas of other theologians.[2]

1 J. Ratzinger, "Newman appartiene ai grandi dottori della Chiesa", in M. K. Strolz, M. Binder (eds.), *John Henry Newman – Lover of Truth* (Urbaniana University Press: 1991), p. 146.

2 Cf. *The Letters and Diaries of John Henry Newman*, Charles Stephen Dessain, Thomas Gornall (eds.), vol. XXIV (Clarendon Press: 1973), pp. 212f.

Although he was made a cardinal by Leo XIII in 1879 and left the world in the odour of sanctity, his writings initially received little attention. At the beginning of the 20th century some representatives of modernism thought that they could draw on his thinking.[3] This is probably why, for several decades, he was not considered in Catholic theology. Only great figures – like Romano Guardini, Erich Przywara, Edith Stein, Theodor Haecker, Henri de Lubac, and Yves Congar – discovered Newman's genius, seeking to enrich theological discussions with Newman's insights. Moreover, through the mediation of eminent theologians Newman's thought was also accepted by the magisterium of the Church. For this reason, Ian Ker, considered one of the greatest experts on Newman's thought, called him the "Father of Vatican II".[4]

The popes in recent decades have repeatedly expressed their profound esteem for the English theologian. "Newman will one day be a Doctor of the Church", Pius XII confided to Jean Guitton.[5] John XXIII cited Newman in his very first encyclical letter, of 29 June 1959, highlighting his significance for the search for Christian unity.[6]

Paul VI spoke a number of times about Newman's relevance. In a speech on 7 April 1975 he noted that Newman "today becomes an ever brighter beacon for all who are seeking an informed orientation and sure guidance amid the uncertainties of the modern world – a world which he himself prophetically foresaw. Many of the problems which he treated with wisdom – although he himself was frequently misunderstood and misinterpreted in his own time – were the subjects of the discussion and study of the Fathers of the Second Vatican Council [...]. Not

3 Cf. for example H. Bremond, *Newman. Essai de biographie psychologique* (Bloud & Cie: 1906).

4 I. Ker, *Newman and the Fullness of Christianity* (T&T Clark Ltd: 1993), p. 127.

5 J. Guitton, *Dialoghi con Paolo VI* (Rusconi: 1986), p. 146.

6 John XXIII, Encyclical letter *Ad Petri Cathedram*, 29 June 1959, Part III.

only this Council but also the present time can be considered in a special way as Newman's hour."[7]

John Paul II also emphasised his affinity with the English theologian on many occasions. At an audience held on 27 April 1990 for a group of Newman friends, he said: "The mystery of the Church always remained the great love of John Henry Newman's life. […] Newman's writings project an eminently clear picture of his unwavering love of the Church as the continuing outpouring of God's love for humanity in every phase of history. His was a truly spiritual vision, capable of perceiving all the weaknesses present in the human fabric of the Church, but equally sure in its perception of the mystery hidden beyond our material gaze."[8]

Benedict XVI had the joy of raising Newman to the honours of the altar on 19 September 2010, in the course of an apostolic journey to England. During a prayer vigil, the beatification Mass, and the Christmas address for that year, he presented the reasons for the particular relevance that Newman has for our time. In his address at the prayer vigil in London's Hyde Park, he said: "In our day, when an intellectual and moral relativism threatens to sap the very foundations of our society, Newman reminds us that, as men and women made in the image and likeness of God, we were created to know the truth, to find in that truth our ultimate freedom and the fulfilment of our deepest human aspirations. In a word, we are meant to know Christ, who is himself 'the way, and the truth, and the life' (*John* 14:6)."[9]

Pope Francis, in addition to canonising Newman on 13 October 2019, expressed many times his esteem and fondness for the English

7 Paul VI, Address to the participants in the Cardinal Newman academic symposium, 7 April 1975. Bracketed ellipses show where author shortened quotations.

8 John Paul II, Address to the participants in the symposium on the centenary of the death of Cardinal John Henry Newman, 27 April 1990.

9 Benedict XVI, Address at the prayer vigil on the eve of the beatification of Cardinal John Henry Newman, 18 September 2010.

cardinal, highlighting the relevance of his thought and action in important statements and speeches.[10]

Considering Newman's influence on theology, his invisible presence at Vatican Council II, and the high esteem in which recent popes have held him, it is not surprising that he was long rumoured to be a possible Doctor of the Church.[11] In conjunction with his canonisation there were also authoritative churchmen, like Canadian cardinal Marc Ouellet, who endorsed this suggestion.[12] The cardinal himself wrote in a greeting to the organisers of an international conference on Newman held in Vienna in October 2021: "The canonisation of Cardinal Newman was for me a welcome opportunity to rediscover his theological work, precisely in its significance for the present hour. He is truly *doctor ecclesiae.*"[13]

What many of the faithful have firmly hoped for and ardently desired is now a reality: on 1 November 2025 Pope Leo numbered St John Henry Newman among the Doctors of the Church, thus highlighting the eminent significance of his teaching.

This book aims to present, in simple terms, some of the most important and timely themes of this new Doctor of the Church, bringing out their relevance to current theological and ecclesial discussion. The various presentations have developed in recent years in the context of my work as director of the International

10 Cf. Francis, Encyclical letter on faith *Lumen Fidei*, 29 June 2013, no. 48; Apostolic exhortation on the proclamation of the Gospel in today's world *Evangelii Gaudium*, 24 November 2013, no. 86; Catechesis during the general audience, 31 May 2017; Address to the bishops ordained over the past year, 14 September 2017; Address to students and teachers of the University of Macerata, 9 May 2022.

11 Cf. for example Ph. Lefebvre, C. Mason (eds.), *John Henry Newman: Doctor of the Church* (Family Publications: 2007).

12 Cf. M. Ouellet, "The Significance of St John Henry Newman for Catholic Theology." This important talk, given on 12 October 2019 during a symposium at the Vatican on the eve of the canonisation, appeared in P. Shrimpton (ed.), *Lead Kindly Light: Essays for Fr Ian Ker* (Gracewing: 2022), pp. 53–66.

13 P. Becker, M. Schlosser, B. Wodrazka (eds.), *John Henry Newman – Welt Gottes und Wahrheit des Menschen* (Herder: 2022), p. 8.

Centre of Newman Friends, established in 1975 by members of the Spiritual Family The Work.

For the sake of understanding Newman's thought the first chapter offers a brief summary of his journey of faith and life. Almost all of his writings arose from a commitment he had made, a service he had to carry out, or an invitation he wanted to accept. For the most part he did not take up his pen without a "call" or "prompting" of this kind.[14] At the centre of his thought, in fact, is not some theory, but the concrete reality of the people of God: the history of the Church amid the challenges of the times, which is the history of God with humanity.

Of particular relevance is Newman's awareness that Christianity is a living truth, of divine origin, that unfolds in the community of the Church, under the guidance of the Holy Spirit, in the course of history. His reflections on the development of Christian doctrine and on the criteria for distinguishing between true and false developments, summarised in the second chapter, are of great interest and can also provide guidance in present-day discussions.

Newman had the firm conviction that the transmission of the faith is entrusted to the whole Church. He therefore emphasised that, in addition to the clear proclamation of the pastors, the courageous witness of the laity is also necessary. His thoughts on the consensus of the faithful, presented in the third chapter, still possess the power to inspire, above all in view of a renewed harmony between pastors and laity, for which he fervently hoped, and of the proper involvement of all the faithful, according to the different charisms and vocations, in the Church's life and mission.

Newman masterfully presented the path of his conversions in his *Apologia Pro Vita Sua*. This classic of modern literature, discussed in the fourth chapter, also has enduring significance. Faith in and love for the Church, in fact, are communicated above all

14 Cf. J.H. Newman, *Autobiographical Writings* (Sheed and Ward: 1957), pp. 272f.

through personal testimony. Furthermore, openness to conversion, prayer, and the search for truth are aspects fundamental for the ecumenical movement.

Newman can also help us to grasp the authentic significance of conscience, while at the same time overcoming one-sided or false understandings. His reflections on this central theme, which form the fifth chapter, emphasise the dignity and primacy of conscience, but also the Church's indispensable role in its proper formation. For Newman conscience is the advocate of truth in the human heart, the aboriginal vicar of Christ: a fascinating view.

Newman strove throughout his life to refute liberalism in religion, highlighting Christianity as a true religion. His sermons on St Paul, presented in the sixth chapter, show that he devoted himself to this service of truth with great sensitivity, sincerity, and delicacy. *Cor ad cor loquitur*: according to this, his motto as cardinal, he was struck by the heart of the Lord, he addressed himself to the heart of his neighbour, and he constantly entrusted his work to the loving heart of the Saviour. Such a message, from heart to heart, can touch people also in our day.

I hope that this book will allow readers to access some of the important writings of St John Henry Newman and will act as an incentive to deepen their study and veneration of this new Doctor of the Church.

Fr Hermann Geissler, FSO

I. A Witness of Faith: Newman's Life and Thought

"I have no tendency to be a saint – it is a sad thing to say so. Saints are not literary men, they do not love the classics, they do not write Tales. I may be well enough in my way, but it is not the 'high line'. [...] It is enough for me to black the saints' shoes – if St Philip uses blacking in heaven."[15] John Henry Newman wrote these words a few years after his conversion, when he heard that someone had called him a saint.

There is no doubt: Newman always thought he was quite far from Christian perfection. On 13 October 2019, nonetheless, Pope Francis numbered him in the company of the saints. The road to this official recognition was long and arduous. Anglicans considered him a traitor because he converted to the Church of Rome. Many Catholics could not comprehend his genius because he was a forerunner of future times and reflected on questions that would only be addressed a hundred years later. Some of his writings, for a while, were even suspected of being heterodox. At the same time, however, Newman was already loved and admired during his lifetime as a theologian, preacher and writer, as a good pastor and spiritual father, as a witness to the truth, a man of conscience and of fidelity to the Church. Who was this theologian and saint? What are the hallmarks of his thought?[16]

15 *The Letters and Diaries of John Henry Newman*, Charles Stephen Dessain (ed.), vol. XIII (Thomas Nelson and Sons Ltd: 1963), p. 419.

16 Among the numerous biographies, we should mention in particular: I. Ker, *John Henry Newman. A Biography* (Clarendon Press: 2010); G. Biemer, *Die Wahrheit wird stärker sein.*

1. The first conversion

Newman was born on 21 February 1801 in the city of London and was baptised into the Church of England. He grew up in a typical middle-class family: his father, John, was a banker and from a religious point of view rather liberal. His mother, Jemima, a descendant of a French Huguenot family that had emigrated to England, was marked by an evangelical-style faith and introduced John Henry, the eldest son, and his five siblings (Charles, Francis, Harriet, Jemima, and Mary) to the religion of the Bible at a young age.

In 1808 Newman's father enrolled him in the private boarding school of Ealing. He soon showed great interest not only in his studies, but also in music – he learned to play the violin – in organisation – he became the leader of a student club – and in literature – he published two magazines called *The Spy* and *The Anti-Spy*. From the religious point of view, in his youth he did not have a solid foundation. Quite early, at the age of fourteen, he read authors like Hume and Voltaire, whose ideas seemed persuasive to him and made him increasingly doubt the existence of God. In his diary, he wrote of this period: "I recollect [...] thinking I should like to be virtuous, but not religious. There was something in the latter idea I did not like. Nor did I see the *meaning* of loving God."[17] (Emphasis is Newman's.) The great temptation of the young Newman was to aim for a good life, but setting God aside.

Amid these inner struggles a great change occurred that he always called his "first conversion". At the time the Newman family unexpectedly found itself in a precarious financial situation

Das Leben Kardinal Newmans (Peter Lang: 2009); F. Morrone, *Con occhi di fede. L'avventura umana e credente di John H. Newman* (Cittadella: 2010); L. Callegari, *John Henry Newman. La ragionevolezza della fede* (Ares: 2010); K. Beaumont, *Comprendre John Henry Newman. Vie et pensée d'un maitre et témoin spirituel* (Saint-Léger: 2015); I. Harrison, *Saint John Henry Newman. His Life and Work* (Catholic Truth Society: 2019).

17 Newman, *Autobiographical Writings*, p. 169.

because of the failure of the father's bank, due to the serious financial crisis following the downfall of Napoleon. So in the summer of 1816 John Henry stayed at the boarding school and, ill, read *The Force of Truth* by Thomas Scott. This book struck him deeply: he came to a lively faith in the presence of God, and at the same time to strong reservations concerning the things of this world. This faith had its effects in isolating him "from the objects which surrounded me, in confirming me in my mistrust of the reality of material phenomena, and making me rest in the thought of two and two only absolute and luminously self-evident beings, myself and my Creator".[18] Newman understood deep down that the invisible world of God and the soul constitutes the decisive reality, which is more real and meaningful than the visible world around us. He moved from a theistic religion, which was put to a hard test, to a properly Christian faith, of evangelical stamp.

From Thomas Scott's book he also borrowed two phrases that for many years became guidelines for his life and his efforts: "Holiness rather than peace" and "Growth the only evidence of life".[19] At the same time, even back then he came to the conviction that "it would be the will of God that I should lead a single life".[20]

In the same year, 1816, Newman read Joseph Milner's *History of the Church of Christ*, which stirred in him a love for the Church Fathers: he was "nothing short of enamoured of the long extracts from St Augustine and the other Fathers", and "read them as being the religion of the primitive Christians".[21] But he was convinced that he had to keep his distance from the Church of Rome, thinking – as many did in England at the time – that the Pope was the Antichrist.

18 J.H. Newman, *Apologia Pro Vita Sua* (Longmans, Green, Reader, and Dyer: 1878), p. 4.

19 Ibid., p. 5.

20 Ibid., p. 7.

21 Ibid.

2. Responsibility for souls

At the age of 16 Newman began his university studies at Trinity College, Oxford. In comparison with Cambridge, the other centre of intellectual excellence, Oxford offered its students a more stable anchoring in the Anglican religious tradition, which claimed a clear ecclesial identity situated between Roman Catholicism and Lutheran Protestantism: Oxford was the university that looked to Christian antiquity as to its very roots.

Immersed in an atmosphere that stimulated his intelligence, Newman, after three years of studies, prepared for his first examination, the Bachelor of Arts. He wanted to get the highest marks, with honours. But although he passed the exam, it was almost a fiasco, as he was near exhaustion. Adding to his personal disappointment was the news of yet more financial ruin for his father. In this period he had to decide on his future. Partly under pressure from his family he revisited an idea that had been on his mind for some time: "My Father this morning said I ought to make up my mind what I was to be. [...] So I chose; and determined on the Church. Thank God, this is what I have prayed for."[22]

At the prestigious Oriel College he wanted to become a fellow, a professor dedicated to study and teaching. He therefore took on a demanding five-day exam, and this time he passed brilliantly. In 1822 – at the age of just 21 – he was thus numbered among the professors of the college, coming into contact with the leading intellectual figures then teaching at Oxford.

In 1824 he became a deacon, and on the day of his ordination he wrote in his diary: "I have the responsibility of souls on me to the day of my death."[23] While in his first conversion he had discovered, by a special grace, the reality of God and of the invisible

22 Newman, *Autobiographical Writings*, p. 180.

23 Ibid., p. 201.

world, here he understood that serving God must include serving others: a responsibility not only for himself, but also for his neighbour. After his ordination as a deacon, along with his teaching duties he set to work in the poor parish of St Clement in Oxford. He began, for example, to visit parishioners in their homes. This pastoral method was novel at the time and shows a fundamental aspect of Newman's personality: his profound conviction that, in bearing witness to human, spiritual, and religious values, much depends on personal contact.

Ordained a priest in 1825, during these early university years Newman came into contact with several colleagues who helped him to overcome the influence of evangelicalism. He learned from Edward Hawkins "to weigh my words, and to be cautious in my statements. [...] Then as to doctrine [...] I was led to give up my remaining Calvinism, and to receive the doctrine of Baptismal Regeneration."[24] From Richard Whately he acquired belief in the Church "as a substantive body or corporation"[25] and an aversion to the Church's subordination to the state. Attending the gatherings of professors of this stamp slowly led him into the orbit of religious liberalism, that is, of the idea that reason was the measure of Revelation. This seduction, however, lasted only until 1827, and religious liberalism would later become the philosophical and theological vision that Newman fought against his whole life.

At Oriel College, meanwhile, his responsibilities increased significantly. In 1826 he was appointed tutor: he was therefore responsible for a group of students to whom he offered assistance of an intellectual nature, but also moral and spiritual. Newman made great efforts on behalf of the students, seeking to shape their minds, their characters, and their consciences.

24 Newman, *Apologia*, pp. 8–9.

25 Ibid., p. 12.

In 1828 he was made vicar of the university church of St Mary in Oxford, a post he would keep until 1843. The sermons that he gave every Sunday evening in this church had a strong impact on his listeners. These are theological and spiritual lectures delivered before a large, culturally diverse audience. They demonstrate his profound faith, his extensive knowledge of Sacred Scripture, and his remarkable ability to enlighten people's consciences.

In those years Newman was studying many works of the 18th-century Anglican tradition, including Bishop Joseph Butler's *Analogy.* From him he learned above all two points that "are the underlying principles of a great portion of my teaching. First, the very idea of an analogy between the separate works of God leads to the conclusion that the system which is of less importance is economically or sacramentally connected with the more momentous system [...]. Secondly, Butler's doctrine that Probability is the guide of life, led me [...] to the question of the logical cogency of Faith."[26]

Also decisive for the development of his religious thought was his friendship with John Keble and Richard Hurrel Froude, two well-known exponents of High Church Anglicanism. To Keble, Newman owed above all the idea of the sacramental system, or the doctrine according to which phenomena are symbols and instruments of invisible realities. Froude imparted to him, despite all his reservations, a certain admiration for the Church of Rome and a decided aversion to the Protestant Reformation, as well as devotion to the Virgin Mary and faith in the real presence of Jesus Christ in the Eucharist. Their fruitful friendship lasted until Froude's sudden death in 1836. Newman was greatly struck by his human, intellectual, and religious personality.

The university parish also included a little village near Oxford, called Littlemore. Newman regularly visited the parishioners of

26 Ibid., pp. 10–11.

this village. He had a church and school built for them, a sign of his constant striving for the formation of both the religious dimension and the intellectual faculties of men. Driven by his responsibility for souls, he sought to connect with every person, to understand their specific situation and to accompany them on their journey. More than twenty thousand letters that he wrote during his long life, collected in thirty-two large volumes, testify to this sense of responsibility, an expression of a profound love of neighbour. It is no coincidence that Newman later chose, as cardinal, the motto *Cor ad cor loquitur*: he felt touched by the heart of God and made great efforts to touch the hearts of others.

3. The search for truth

In 1828 Newman began systematically to read the Church Fathers, reading that would later decisively mark his path. He had already studied Sacred Scripture through and through. Now the treasury of Tradition to which the Fathers bore witness was also opened up for him. At that time he prepared his first study, on the history of the Arians of the fourth century, and consolidated his conviction that the Church of the early centuries constituted the faithful interpretation of Christian doctrine. What particularly attracted him "was the great Church of Alexandria, the historical centre of teaching in those times. [...] Athanasius, the champion of the truth, was Bishop of Alexandria; and in his writings he refers to the great religious names of an earlier date, to Origen, Dionysius, and others, who were the glory of its see, or of its school. The broad philosophy of Clement and Origen carried me away."[27]

In 1832, disillusioned by the growing influence of religious liberalism at Oxford and worn out from his book on *The Arians of the Fourth Century*, Newman decided to take, with a few friends, a trip across the Mediterranean. He visited Rome and also went

[27] Ibid., p. 26.

to Sicily, where he became gravely ill: "I struck into the middle of the island, and fell ill of a fever at Leonforte. My servant thought that I was dying, and begged for my last directions. I gave them, as he wished; but I said, 'I shall not die.' I repeated, 'I shall not die, for I have not sinned against light, I have not sinned against light.' I never have been able to make out at all what I meant."[28] During this illness Newman saw in the depths of his soul that he had served the Lord and his neighbour, but he also took note of his pride and felt the pressing call to give himself to God with more humility and to follow his plan with more fidelity. After his recovery, returning to England, he wrote the famous poem "Lead, Kindly Light", in which he gave expression to the experience he had lived through during his illness in Sicily. He was determined to abandon himself entirely to God's guidance.

To combat religious liberalism in Oxford and throughout England, in 1833 Newman and some of his friends began the "Oxford Movement". They took their cue from a famous sermon that John Keble preached at the university church of St Mary, on national apostasy: England, Keble said, had lost its faith and needed a "second Reformation": a renewal in the spirit of early Christianity.

Newman summarised the Movement's three principles in these words: "First was the principle of dogma: my battle was with liberalism; by liberalism I mean the anti-dogmatic principle and its developments."[29] The second was the sacramental principle, the belief in the existence of a visible Church, with sacraments that constitute the channels of invisible grace. The third was the anti-Roman principle: against the accusation of "popery", soon levelled at the promoters of the Oxford Movement, Newman defended himself by asserting that the Church of Rome had bound itself to the cause of the Antichrist.

28 Ibid., pp. 34–35.
29 Ibid., p. 48.

The Oxford Movement sought to promote a true reform of the Church of England. Through intense preaching and the publication of *Tracts for the Times*, easily disseminated treatises, its promoters sought to penetrate the consciences of clergymen and lay faithful alike, caught between two extremes: on the one hand sentimentalism and fideism and on the other increasingly widespread rationalism. Newman realised that the polemic against religious liberalism needed a good doctrinal foundation. He was convinced that he had found it in the writings of the Church Fathers, whom he admired as the real heralds of the truth.

In his desire to put the Church of England back on the course of the most authentic Christian tradition, he aimed to strengthen the theological foundations of Anglicanism by developing the theory of the *Via Media*. According to this theory the Protestants had abandoned parts of the primitive Creed, the Romans instead had sullied the purity of the faith with the addition of errors and superstitions, while the Anglicans had remained faithful to the tradition of the primitive Church within the balance of the *Via Media*.

In those years of intense activity Newman published the eight volumes of the famous parish sermons (*Parochial and Plain Sermons*). He gave a series of lectures, subsequently published, on questions of ecclesiology (*On the Prophetical Office of the Church, Via Media, vol. II*), on the theology of justification and grace (*Lectures on Justification*), and on the relationship between faith and reason (*University Sermons*). Above all, with the book *On the Prophetical Office of the Church* he sought to contribute to the formation of official Anglican theology, basing his argument on the Tradition and doctrine of the primitive Church.

A sincere search for the truth always characterised Newman's speculative inquiry and spiritual efforts; as a result, he gradually had to admit the flimsiness of the theory of the *Via Media*. Is truth always found in the middle? Studying the troubled history of the fourth-century Church, Newman made a disturbing discovery: he found the Christianity of his century reflected in the three groups of that time – in the Arians, the Protestants; in the Romans, the Church of Rome; in the Semi-Arians, the Anglicans.

Shortly afterward he was struck by a phrase of St Augustine: *Securus iudicat orbem terrarum*, or, in Newman's translation: "The deliberate judgement, in which the whole Church at length rests and acquiesces, is an infallible prescription."[30] He understood that in the ancient Church doctrinal conflicts were resolved not only on the basis of antiquity but also on the basis of catholicity: the judgement of the whole Church is an infallible decree. Newman had to acknowledge that the Church of England was not universal (catholic), but national. Consequently, "the theory of the *Via Media* was absolutely pulverised."[31]

In 1841 he published *Tract 90*, an attempt to explain what are called the Thirty-Nine Articles, the foundation of the Anglican Creed, in a Catholic vein, starting from the Church Fathers. But the treatise was condemned by the university council and then by the bishops of the Church of England, while students were urged to desert St Mary's Church when Newman was preaching.

4. The drama of the conversion

Faithful to his principle of always honouring the truth, Newman decided to withdraw, along with some friends, to Littlemore, on the outskirts of Oxford, for a period of research, prayer, and study. In 1843 he recanted all his accusations against the Church of Rome, which until then he had considered bound to the cause of the Antichrist. He also resigned, with deep regret, from his position as an Anglican minister.

Praying and studying, Newman was increasingly drawn to the Church of Rome, but he was not yet convinced that he had

30 Ibid., p. 117.

31 Ibid.

to convert. His great question was this: if the Roman Catholic Church is in apostolic continuity, what justification is there for those doctrines that do not appear to be part of the heritage of faith of early Christianity, like the doctrine of purgatory, the veneration of Mary and the saints, the primacy of the Pope? At the end of 1844 he began an in-depth study to determine to what extent his new convictions were grounded in the Tradition of the ancient Church, and by virtue of what inner logic within the dynamism of ecclesial faith and life the developments brought about by Rome were theologically justifiable. While prayer brought an increasingly convinced openness to the Church of Rome, he felt the need to further clarify the grounds of reason that his journey of faith had already intuited. His troubled experience of faith had to be communicable to his friends and to those who disapproved of his journey. The fruit of these reflections, together with no few sufferings, was the famous *Essay on the Development of Christian Doctrine*.

As Newman proceeded with this study he understood that the Church of Rome was in perfect continuity with the Church of the Fathers, the Church of the apostles, the Church of Christ. He therefore wrote in the *Apologia*: "As I advanced, my difficulties so cleared away that I ceased to speak of 'the Roman Catholics,' and boldly called them Catholics. Before I got to the end, I resolved to be received, and the book remains in the state in which it was then, unfinished."[32]

Here one sees Newman's consistency: when in conscience he recognised something as a duty he immediately took the appropriate steps; thus he carried out in his life what he wrote in his essay on the development of Christian doctrine: "In a higher world it is otherwise, but here below to live is to change, and to be perfect is to have changed often."[33] Newman's conversion was not an

32 Ibid., p. 234.

33 J.H. Newman, *An Essay on the Development of Christian Doctrine* (Basil Montagu Pickering: 1878), p. 40.

arbitrary change but the logical consequence of his first conversion and the expression of his fidelity to the kindly light that had always led him.

On 9 October 1845 he was received into the Catholic Church by the Italian Passionist Dominic Barberi, who was later beatified by Pope Paul VI in 1963. At the age of 44 Newman left the Church of England and therefore also his friends, his profession, his career. He converted to the Church of Rome, in his day a small group of faithful on the fringes of English society. For him this transition was not a matter of personal sentiment or taste, but of obedience to the truth, revealed little by little in his conscience. Like St Thomas More, Newman followed the call of his conscience, considering it to be more important than success, prestige, and public approval. In him we can admire a true man of conscience, who, following the imperative of this inner voice, found peace: "From the time that I became a Catholic [... I] have had no anxiety of heart whatever. I have been in perfect peace and contentment; I never have had one doubt. [...] [I]t was like coming into port after a rough sea; and my happiness on that score remains to this day without interruption."[34]

5. Trials and sufferings

A few months after his entrance into the Catholic Church, Newman, together with his friend Ambrose St John, moved to Rome, to the College of *Propaganda Fide*, where he was ordained a priest on 30 May 1847.

During this stay in Rome he also learned about St Philip Neri, who was much to his liking, and he decided to become an Oratorian. With the Pope's approval and after a brief novitiate he and a group of friends founded the first English Oratory in Birmingham, adapting the statutes to the English mentality. For

34 Newman, *Apologia*, p. 238.

the rest of his life he spent most of his time in the Birmingham Oratory, where he developed a rich pastoral ministry with his confreres, accompanied many people on their journey of faith, founded a school, and continued his intense theological work.

Newman sought to contribute to the religious formation of Catholics in England, composed of working-class Irish and a growing number of new converts, all in need of intellectual and spiritual support in the faith. In 1848 he published an autobiographical novel (*Loss and Gain: The Story of a Convert*), in defence of his move to Catholicism. In 1850, the year in which the Catholic hierarchy was re-established in England, he gave lectures in London to illustrate the reasons for the Catholic faith in the face of the dogmatic and moral difficulties that the Anglicans were posing to the reborn Catholic community (*Lectures on Certain Difficulties Felt by Anglicans in Submitting to the Catholic Church*). A series of lectures followed in Birmingham on the current situation of Catholics in England, unmasking the prejudice against the Church of Rome and explaining its claim to truth (*Lectures on the Present Position of Catholics in England*). Newman thus became the spiritual and intellectual leader of English Catholics. Not by chance, the bishops asked him to give the homily at the first Synod of the newly re-established English Catholic hierarchy.

But during that period, despite the joy of having found the haven of the Catholic Church, Newman had to endure one trial after another. In public opinion many doubted his personal integrity: they were unable to understand how such an intelligent man could have left the Church of England, joining a small group of Catholics. Among Anglicans he was considered a traitor, and many Catholics had trouble understanding his genius. Moreover, Newman had to endure misunderstanding, suspicion, and even slander. We can mention only a few of these experiences.

In 1851 Newman was called by the bishops of Ireland to found a Catholic university in Dublin, a wonderful opportunity for the former tutor of Oriel College to regain the leading role worthy of his genius. He was appointed its first rector and prepared a series of addresses, afterward published under the title *The Idea of a University*, another classic work. According to him, the Catholic university was to provide Catholics, particularly the laity, with the means of culture and of the formation of a generous elite, open to the problems of the time, capable of integrating into society in order to take on an important role in it. But his ideas were not shared by the bishops, who wanted a defensive and clerical university. After many disappointments, in 1858 Newman realised that the project had failed and had to resign as rector.

That same year the English bishops approached him with a new and difficult but fascinating task: a new English translation of the Bible. He eagerly set about the work and found good collaborators. But a short time later he learned that the American bishops were also preparing an English translation of Scripture and that the English bishops had abandoned the project without informing him. So he had to stand down from his role.

In 1859 he accepted the post of editor of *The Rambler*. He saw this magazine as an opportunity to provide a platform for Catholic thinking that had not yet managed to express itself in a balanced and generous way. Enjoying undisputed intellectual prestige, Newman was able to offer Catholics a forum for dialogue between faith and culture. In 1859 he published two articles on the role of the laity in the Church, asserting, with the necessary theological clarifications and with solid historical argument, that they have the right to affirm the consensus of their faith on doctrinal questions. After these articles, which are of unquestionable orthodoxy, some prelates denounced him, and his bishop asked him to resign from the editorship of the *Rambler*.

But the matter was not yet closed. The aforementioned articles were reported to Rome. Some questions from *Propaganda Fide* did not make it to Newman, and for a few years he was even suspected of heresy. Moreover, certain prelates of the ultramontane faction portrayed Newman as unreliable. Monsignor George Talbot, prelate of the Antechamber of the Apostolic Palace, famously remarked, "Dr Newman is the most dangerous man in England."[35] All these suspicions had no foundation at all but were the fruit of intrigue and slander.

6. Rehabilitation and fundamental commitment

In 1864 Charles Kingsley, a professor of modern history at Cambridge, published an article questioning the sincerity of the Catholic clergy, and especially of Dr Newman. To defend the Catholic clergy and the Catholic Church itself Newman wrote, within a few weeks, a history of his religious views, afterward published under the title *Apologia Pro Vita Sua*. With the *Apologia* he regained popularity and respect on the part of all. Catholics, and priests above all, understood that Newman was their best defender. Anglicans had to admit that Newman, despite leaving the Church of England, had sincerely followed the dictates of his conscience. And English citizens admired the beauty of his language. Indeed it can be said that since the schism caused by Henry VIII in 1534 the *Apologia* was the first book written by a Catholic to be read by many people in all of England.

In the following years Newman wrote other highly significant essays. In 1865, after the sudden death of a friend, he published a short eschatological poem in which he describes the soul's journey from the deathbed to the judgement seat of God and finally to purgatory (*The Dream of Gerontius*). Later Edward Elgar set it to music and presented *The Dream of Gerontius* as an oratorio.

In 1866 Newman responded to Pusey, a brother in arms from the Oxford Movement who had remained in the bosom of

35 W. Ward, *The Life of John Henry Cardinal Newman*, vol. II (Longmans, Green, and Co.: 1913), p. 147.

Anglicanism, on the devotion of Catholics to Mary. In this essay he offers a historical-salvific Mariology based on the theology of the Church Fathers, presenting Mary first of all as the "new Eve".

In 1870 he published the *Essay in Aid of a Grammar of Assent*, the mature fruit of long reflection on the relationship between faith and reason, which had always interested Newman. In this book, another classic, he analyses the act of the assent of the human mind to truth, seeking to defend the right to certainty on matters of faith, even if it's not possible to demonstrate it scientifically.

In 1875 Newman published the *Letter to the Duke of Norfolk*, motivated by former prime minister Gladstone's assertion that Catholics, after the definition of the dogma of papal infallibility (1870), could no longer be loyal citizens. To respond to this accusation Newman wrote a long essay in which he clarified in a balanced way the relationship between the authority of conscience and that of the Church and the Pope. This work too is of great relevance.

Newman's definitive rehabilitation took place with the consistory of 15 May 1879, at which Pope Leo XIII, newly elected to the chair of Peter, elevated him to the dignity of cardinal.

Upon receiving the "biglietto" for his election to the cardinalate, Newman, looking back on his past life, said among other things: "In a long course of years I have made many mistakes. I have nothing of that high perfection, which belongs to the writings of Saints, viz: that error cannot be found in them; but what I trust that I may claim all through what I have written, is this, – an honest intention, an absence of private ends, a temper of obedience, a willingness to be corrected, a dread of error, a desire to serve Holy Church, and, through Divine Mercy, a fair measure of success."[36] The cardinal elect then summarised the fundamental effort of his

36 Newman, *Speech of His Eminence Cardinal Newman on the Reception of the "Biglietto"* (Libreria Spithöver: 1879), p. 6.

life: "And I rejoice to say, to one great mischief I have from the first opposed myself. For 30, 40, 50 years I have resisted to the best of my powers the spirit of liberalism in religion."[37] He thus alluded to the unity of purpose that had inspired his whole life, both as an Anglican and as a Catholic. Although open to the problems of the time, he had always resisted what he called religious liberalism: "Liberalism in religion is the doctrine that there is no positive truth in religion, but that one creed is as good as another, and this is the teaching which is gaining substance and force daily. It is inconsistent with any recognition of any religion, as *true*. It teaches that all are to be tolerated, but all are matters of opinion. Revealed religion is not a truth, but a sentiment and a taste; not an objective fact; not miraculous: and it is the right of each individual to make it say just what strikes his fancy. Devotion is not necessarily founded on faith. [...] Since then, religion is so personal a peculiarity and so private a possession, we must of necessity ignore it in the intercourse of man with man."[38] (Emphasis is Newman's.)

These words describe today's mentality, called "relativism" by Benedict XVI and "indifferentism" by Pope Francis. With prophetic vision Newman had foreseen this danger looming over the Church. But he added that, in spite of all the challenges, we must not become discouraged, because the Lord remains with his Church, and Christians must not think they have more influence if they conform to the spirit of the world. Such "worldly Christianity" makes itself superfluous. One must trust not in the world, but in the Lord, according to the concluding words of Newman's aforementioned speech: "Christianity has been too often in what seemed deadly peril that we should fear for it any new trial now. [...] Commonly the Church has nothing more to

37 Ibid.

38 Ibid., p. 7.

do than to go on in her own proper duties, in confidence and peace; to stand still and to see the salvation of God."[39]

Newman died on 11 August 1890 in Birmingham. Thousands of faithful attended his funeral. The *London Times* published a lengthy obituary, concluding: "Of one thing we may be sure, that the memory of his pure and noble life, untouched by worldliness, unsoured by any trace of fanaticism, will endure, and that whether Rome canonises him or not he will be canonised in the thoughts of pious people of many creeds in England."[40]

The canonisation process officially began in 1958, during the pontificate of Pius XII. After Vatican Council II the Spiritual Family The Work – together with the Oratorians – contributed to promoting the veneration of Newman, above all with the organisation of the first academic symposium on Newman in Rome (1975) and the foundation of various Newman Centres in Rome, Littlemore/Oxford, Bregenz, and Budapest. Paul VI personally committed himself to the continuation of the canonisation process. In 1991 John Paul II, another admirer of Newman, was able to sign the decree on his heroic virtues. A few years later, in the archdiocese of Boston, Deacon Jack Sullivan was healed of an incurable spinal disorder through Newman's intercession. This miracle paved the way for his beatification, which Benedict XVI celebrated in England on 19 September 2010. As a rule Benedict XVI delegated the beatification ceremonies. He himself beatified only two people: John Henry Newman and John Paul II. This fact clearly demonstrates his great esteem for the English theologian. Subsequently, after Melissa Villalobos, who was expecting her fifth child and was about to lose the baby due to serious pregnancy difficulties,

39 Ibid., p. 10.

40 *Eminent Persons: Biographies Reprinted from the Times, vol. IV* (Macmillan and Co.: 1893), pp. 275–276.

received a miracle thanks to Newman's help, Pope Francis canonised him on 13 October 2019, in St Peter's Square.

Today Newman is appreciated, venerated, and studied by many people all over the world, well beyond the confines of the Catholic Church. His theology, firmly anchored in Revelation, attentive to the treasury of Tradition and to the developments of the deposit of faith in history, and unafraid of the questions of today's world, is capable of building bridges and pointing out new paths. Newman, declared a Doctor of the Church by Pope Leo XIII on 1 November 2025, is one of the great witnesses of faith who, through their lives and writings, touch our hearts and enlighten our thinking.

II. A Living Truth: The Development of Christian Doctrine

On the occasion of the 25th anniversary of the promulgation of the *Catechism of the Catholic Church*, celebrated on 11 October 2017, Pope Francis gave a long address, emphasising among other things that the Church's doctrine is a dynamic reality that develops until the end of time: "Tradition is a living reality and only a partial vision regards the 'deposit of faith' as something static. [...] The word of God is a dynamic and living reality that develops and grows because it is aimed at a fulfilment that none can halt. This law of progress [...] is a distinguishing mark of revealed truth as it is handed down by the Church, and in no way represents a change in doctrine."[41]

In speaking of the progress of doctrine Francis often referred to Vincent of Lérins, who wrote in his *Commonitorium*: "But perhaps someone will say: Will there then be no progress of religion in the Church of Christ? There certainly will be, and to the utmost. For who is so inimical to men, so hateful of God, that he would try to prevent this? But yet in such a way that it be truly progress of the faith, not change. For it belongs to progress that each thing develop in itself, but to change that something be turned from one thing into another."[42] The Christian religion experiences a

41 Francis, Address to the participants in the meeting promoted by the Pontifical Council for Promoting the New Evangelization, 11 October 2017.

42 R. St. Moxon (ed.), *The Commonitorium of Vincentius of Lerins* (Cambridge University Press: 1915), p. 88. Cf. for example, Francis, *Interview by Antonio Spadaro*, 19 August 2013; Encyclical letter *Laudato Si': On Care for Our Common Home*, 24 May 2015,

constant progress (*profectus*), which, however, must not be confused with a change or alteration (*permutatio*).

The aim of this chapter is to show how these two aspects – the reality of progress as an intrinsic aspect of revealed truth, and the criteria for discerning between authentic developments and alterations – were masterfully elaborated by John Henry Newman in the most dramatic phase of his life. As an Anglican minister and professor at Oxford University he had sought to contribute to the renewal of the Christian faith in England, above all through the Oxford Movement. His aspirations to renew the Church of England in the spirit of the Fathers, however, met with growing opposition from its official representatives. These events caused him tremendous problems of conscience, as he could not and would not work for a community whose fundamental beliefs he no longer shared. So in 1842 he withdrew to Littlemore to devote himself entirely to the search for the true Church. At the end of 1844 he decided to write *An Essay on the Development of Christian Doctrine*.

1. Context

From February to October 1845 Newman wrote almost non-stop. Why did he take on this project?[43] By then he had already realised on the one hand that he could no longer remain in the Church of England, believing that, as a national Church, it was not really catholic. On the other hand he was not yet able to join the Roman Catholic Church, whose doctrines, developed over time, he had

no. 121; Press conference during the return flight from Rabat to Rome, 21 March 2019; Address to the participants in the international conference: "Lines of development of the global compact on education", 1 June 2022; Press conference during the return flight from Canada, 29 July 2022.

43 All Newman biographies describe the context of this essay and underline its importance. Cf. for example Ker, *John Henry Newman. A Biography*, pp. 257–315; Biemer, *Die Wahrheit wird stärker sein*, pp. 189–201; Callegari, *John Henry Newman. La ragionevolezza della fede*, pp. 244–252.

long rejected as non-apostolic. Many questions were nagging at him: how to evaluate Catholic "innovations", as, for example, Marian devotion, the veneration of angels and saints, prayers for the deceased, the doctrine on the papacy? He asked himself: are these doctrines and practices symptoms of infidelity and corruption with respect to the original faith? Are they arbitrary additions made for purely human motives? Or are they perhaps expressions of an organic development of the deposit of faith, entrusted to the Church by Jesus Christ and his apostles?

A strong need of conscience drove Newman to clarify these questions in order to find light for his path. The questions, however, did not only concern his personal future; he also felt the responsibility of the theologian who must account, also with solid arguments, for the ways in which the deposit of faith is transmitted and grows in the course of history. He understood that the history of Revelation itself, as Sacred Scripture bears witness, presents various developments. Was it not therefore likely – he wondered – that there should also be developments in the history of the Church and its doctrine? And if so, how can genuine developments be distinguished from deviations?

Passionate inquiry, intense prayer, and a monastic rhythm of life characterised these dramatic months in Newman's life, spent with some friends at the "College" of Littlemore. The result of his intellectual and spiritual struggle was his conversion to the Catholic Church, which took place on 9 October 1845, even before the definitive completion of his essay.

It is impossible to separate *An Essay on the Development of Christian Doctrine* from the circumstances in which it was born, as it is the study of an Anglican arguing the reasons why he can no longer remain one. It is founded on a basic concept not unknown to traditional theology, whether Anglican or Catholic: that is, the concept of "development", but it can be said that Newman almost reinvents this concept, making it a "decisive criterion for the total interpretation of the Christian fact in time".[44] He shows that the Christian fact exists only "in time" and that Christians must continually convert to this real form of Christianity. In this perspective every believer is called to a permanent conversion in the biblical sense of metanoia. "Growth [is] the only evidence of life."[45] This motto, which Newman adopted back during his first conversion, applies not only to the individual Christian but also to the entire ecclesial community. If the Church does not grow and develop, it does not live. Growth, renewal, and development are signs of life.

2. *Essential content*

It is not easy to summarise the rich and varied ideas of Newman's essay, which fills more than four hundred pages. These considerations are limited to presenting the essential contours of the contents and the common thread of the two parts of the text.[46]

44 A. Prandi, *Introduzione*, in Newman, *Lo sviluppo della dottrina cristiana* (Jaca Book: 2003), p. 14. Siebenrock understands Newman's essay not so much as an "apologia of his conversion" or "strict theory for the development of dogma", but rather as an "*interpretatio historiae*", which "provides essential elements for a self-understanding of Christianity". Cf. R. Siebenrock, *Wahrheit, Gewissen und Geschichte. Eine systematisch-theologische Rekonstruktion des Wirkens John Henry Kardinal Newmans* (Internationale Cardinal-Newman-Studien, Volume 15; Glock und Lutz: 1996), pp. 351–352.

45 Newman, *Apologia*, p. 5.

46 Newman's essay has been the object of many studies. Cf. for example J. Guitton, *La philosophie du Newman. La notion de développement et son application à la religion chez J.H. Newman* (Boivin et Cie, éditeurs: 1933); J.H. Walgrave, *Newman. Le développement du dogme* (Casterman: 1957); O. Chadwick, *From Bossuet to Newman. The Idea of Doctrinal Development* (Cambridge University Press: 1957); N. Lash, *Change in Focus. A Study of Doctrinal Change and Continuity* (Sheed and Ward: 1973); L. Scheffczyk, *Newmans Theorie der Dogmenentwicklung im Lichte der Neueren Kritik* (self-published: 1985); A. Nichols, *From Newman to Congar. The Idea of Doctrinal Development from the Victorians to the Second Vatican Council* (T&T Clark: 1990); Siebenrock, *Wahrheit, Gewissen und Geschichte*, op. cit.; J. Graf, *Von Schatten und Bildern zur Wahrheit. Die Erschließung der "Offenbarung" bei John Henry Newman* (Peter Lang: 2009); M. Seewald, *Il dogma in divenire. Equilibrio dinamico di continuità e discontinuità* (Queriniana: 2020). In this summary presentation of the basic contours of the essay, the quotes are largely limited to those of Newman himself.

2.1 Reality of doctrinal development

The starting point of Newman's theory "is given by the distinctive conception of Christian truth as a living idea which is identical with the original Revelation". This living idea "is not, however, an abstract subjective knowledge, but a living objective totality, an organism containing within itself a great number of elements and aspects, and which develops in time".[47] For Newman the Incarnation is "the central aspect of Christianity",[48] an event that contains within itself the entire Revelation of the Lord. This idea presents itself as so living, fruitful, and supernatural that the human spirit is not able to grasp it all at once. It must instead draw upon it in the course of history and see to it that it reaches its perfection. Starting from this approach, in the first part of the essay Newman examines "doctrinal developments viewed in themselves".[49] He justifies the existence of such developments with two main arguments.

In the first argument he shows that doctrinal developments are presumable ("antecedent argument").[50] Christianity, especially in the central idea of the Incarnation, is destined to develop. This idea, which contains a divine message and surpasses all human knowledge, is revealed so as to be imprinted in the hearts of believers, to permeate the ecclesial community in all places and at all times, to be explained and explored by the human mind, and to permeate the field of the world, as Jesus proclaimed in the para-

47 L. Scheffczyk, *Dogmatica Cattolica, vol. 1: Fondamenti del dogma. Introduzione alla dogmatica* (Lateran University Press: 2010), p. 196. Scheffcyzk offers a good summary of Newman's essential thinking on the development of dogma.

48 Newman, *Development of Christian Doctrine*, p. 36. This Christocentric approach has been explored by various 20th-century theologians and is now part of the doctrine of the Church. Vatican Council II teaches in the dogmatic constitution on divine revelation *Dei Verbum* that Christ "is both the mediator and the fullness of all revelation" (no. 2).

49 Ibid., p. xiii.

50 Ibid., chap. II.

bles about the kingdom of God. Christian Revelation, in fact, is not something static, like a piece of gold that is passed down from generation to generation, but rather something dynamic, like a tree that has within itself a great capacity, constantly receives nourishment, grows and produces new branches and twigs. It is the mystery of Jesus Christ himself that becomes ever more explicit.[51]

Also presumable – Newman continues – is the existence of an infallible authority. If there are doctrinal developments, and this is to be supposed, the question arises of how such developments can be recognised and authenticated as genuine. A tree can produce fruitful branches but also wild shoots. Who in the Church can distinguish between true and false developments? This voice, according to Newman, cannot be Sacred Scripture, because it is open to various interpretations. Nor can it be the ancient Church, as he himself had thought for many years, because this is not a living voice. So he comes to this conclusion: "If Christianity is both social and dogmatic, and intended for all ages, it must humanly speaking have an infallible expounder."[52] Only the existence of such an infallible interpreter can guarantee the unity of the ecclesial community and the faithful preservation and transmission of Revelation. Newman does not yet specify who is the subject of this infallible authority, but he affirms that such an authority must exist within the organism of the Church.

As his second argument Newman maintains that the course of history presents numerous developments that show how expectations have become reality ("historical argument").[53] He points

51 G. Lettieri describes Newman's theology of history "as mystical Christology. The historical development of the idea of the divine identity explicated through the different created intelligences can be interpreted as *kenosis*, the incarnation of the Logos of grace in the historical body of human intelligences and freedoms." Cf. *Postfazione: Newman Alessandrino*, in Newman, *Sviluppo della dottrina*, p. 440.

52 Newman, *Development of Christian Doctrine*, p. 90. It should be emphasised that here Newman is presenting an argument for the infallibility of the Church as such.

53 Ibid., chap. III.

out how some aspects of doctrine have been preserved and transmitted in a rather "implicit" way (spontaneous, not reflective, in prayer and actions). Various concrete circumstances, and not rarely confrontation with heresies, have then brought it about that these aspects have become more evident, have been formulated "explicitly" and in clear terms through theological study, and have finally been defined as truths of faith by the Church's magisterium. This has led to real and proper doctrinal developments in which the community of the faithful, theologians, and the successors of the apostles as subjects of the magisterium of the Church have participated. These developments have helped the faithful to have a better understanding of Revelation than in the previous period, but they have not led to a different faith, because the new doctrines were contained in seminal form in the original Revelation and only made new aspects of its central idea explicit.[54]

Newman illustrates these general considerations with various concrete examples. He shows among other things how in the first centuries – amid numerous heterodox positions – the doctrine on Jesus Christ was developed, and how finally the dignity and mission of Mary were also clearly recognised. His thoughts culminate in this sentence: "In order to do honour to Christ, in order to defend the true doctrine of the Incarnation, in order to secure a right faith in the manhood of the Eternal Son, the Council of Ephesus determined the Blessed Virgin to be the Mother of God."[55] In other words: the veneration of Mary as Mother of God stands in service of faith in Jesus Christ, Son of God, who became incarnate

54 Cf. Scheffczyk, *Dogmatica Cattolica, vol. I*, p. 197. A. Nichols shows well how Newman's thinking on the development from "implicit" aspects to "explicit" formulations matured in the course of the research with which he prepared the essay on the development of Christian doctrine. Cf. Nichols, *From Newman to Congar*, pp. 26–45.

55 Newman, *Development of Christian Doctrine*, p. 145. Newman's historical research is generally well-founded, despite his unfamiliarity as yet with critical editions of the writings of the Church Fathers.

in Mary for the salvation of humanity. Even if this doctrine was explicitly defined only by the Council of Ephesus (431), Newman finds implicit clues to Mary's role in salvation history already in Sacred Scripture, in some very ancient prayers, and in the texts of various ecclesiastical writers of the second and third centuries who present Mary as the "new Eve".

Another example that Newman illustrates in detail is the development of the doctrine of papal primacy. In the first ages of the Church, according to the Oxford theologian, the authority of the bishop of Rome could "sleep".[56] In the post-apostolic period the monarchical principle soon developed: one bishop as head of one diocese. Bit by bit, as Christianity spread, the period of persecution ended, and the difficulties assumed greater proportions, the principle of ecclesiastical unity, presumable from the beginning, was unfolded more and more. When in the fifth century it became necessary this principle then emerged clearly with Leo the Great, who by intervening with the Fathers of the Council of Chalcedon (451) played a decisive role in preserving the Church in the genuine faith in Jesus Christ. In retrospect Newman recognises that this principle of unity is founded on various statements of the Lord to Peter and is already mentioned, though often implicitly, by a multitude of ecclesiastical writers over the centuries.

Examples of this kind are for Newman clear indications that the presumable developments have found their authentic expression in the doctrinal decisions of councils and popes. He is struck by the unity, harmony, and coherence of Catholic doctrine. He sees the faith of the Church as a unitary body formed around the Apostles' Creed and feels supported by the Church Fathers themselves: "Did St. Athanasius or St. Ambrose come suddenly to life, it cannot be doubted what communion he would mistake for his own."[57]

56 Ibid., p. 150.

57 Ibid., p. 97.

The common thread of the first part of Newman's essay could be summarised in the following statements: (1) The central idea of Christianity is the Incarnation, in which the fullness of Revelation is given: Jesus Christ, the truth in person. (2) This central idea is destined to develop in the community of believers; developments are therefore presumable, as is the existence of an infallible authority. (3) The developments that have actually taken place show that the developments to be expected have become reality in the course of history.

2.2 Criteria for discernment

At the beginning of the second part of his essay Newman formulates a radical objection: "It may be said in answer to me [...] that the causes which stimulate the growth of ideas may also disturb and deform them; and that Christianity might indeed have been intended by its Divine Author for a wide expansion of the ideas proper to it, and yet this great benefit hindered by the evil birth of cognate errors which acted as its counterfeit; in a word, that what I have called developments in the Roman Church are nothing more or less than what used to be called her corruptions."[58] To answer this objection Newman elaborates seven criteria of discernment, which he then applies to existing developments in Christian doctrine, convinced that in this way he can distinguish between true developments and corruptions. These extensive historical investigations, which are supported by quotations from a great number of authors, form the "heart of the essay".[59] For Newman the seven criteria are sufficient to decide his fundamental question but do not claim to be exhaustive.

58 Ibid., pp. 169–170. It is clear that for Newman the argument of authority alone, as criterion for discerning true from false developments, is not sufficient. He feels the need to find other criteria of discernment and verification, comprehensible to the logic of faith.

59 Siebenrock, *Wahrheit, Gewissen und Geschichte*, p. 407.

A first distinguishing criterion is "preservation of type".[60] Newman refers by analogy to the human organism, which changes in different ways as it develops from infant to child, to adolescent, to adult, and finally to elder, but remains identical in its fundamental form. He sees the development of the organism of the Church in a similar way: even if different forms of expression grow and develop over time, its general physiognomy – its "type" – remains.[61] In three long sections on the Church of the first centuries, he elaborates three aspects that characterise this general physiognomy: its message coming from God, which was combatted by the pagans as superstition because it could not be integrated into the state religion; its catholic character, which distinguished it from the sects and made it recognisable as a universal community; its connection to the bishop of Rome, who in times of confusion (for example, at the time of the Council of Chalcedon) offered a sure orientation. According to Newman, genuine developments, unlike false ones, are characterised by the fact that with them the type of Church – with its supernatural, catholic, and Roman character – remains preserved.

As the second criterion Newman mentions "continuity of principles".[62] While type instead concerns the external physiognomy of the ecclesiastical organism, principles shape its life and doctrine from within.[63] Generally these principles, while rooted in the central idea of Christianity, the Incarnation, can only be known in the course of history. Doctrines develop; principles must remain the same. If doctrines are torn from their underlying

60 Newman, *Development of Christian Doctrine*, chap. V, sec. I.

61 The concept of "type" is original and not easily understood. It seems that for Newman it means above all the general physiognomy, as seen from the outside and described in almost phenomenological terms.

62 Ibid., sec. II.

63 The concept of "principles" is also complex. According to Newman, principles are comparable to the internal forces that animate and enliven an organism.

principles they can be interpreted in different ways and lead to conflicting conclusions. The continuity of principles is therefore fundamental. Newman highlights four principles in particular: according to the "principle of *dogma*", Christianity concerns "supernatural truths" which – while imperfect in human language – are "definitive and necessary because given from above".[64] According to the "principle of *faith*",[65] it is necessary, with the help of grace, to give an interior assent to the divine Word and to revealed truths. The "principle of *theology*"[66] affirms that the truths received in faith must be scrutinised and explored by reason. The "*sacramental* principle"[67] means that there are visible signs that express and communicate an invisible divine gift.[68] (Emphases are Newman's.) At the end of this chapter Newman notes: "While the development of doctrine in the Church has been in accordance with, or in consequence of these immemorial principles, the various heresies, which have from time to time arisen, have in one respect or other [...] violated those principles [...]. The Gnostics [...] professed to substitute knowledge [...]. The dogmatic rule [...] was thrown aside by all those sects which [...] claimed to judge for themselves from Scripture; and the sacramental principle was violated, *ipso facto*, by all who separated from the Church."[69] It is clear that continuity of principles is a criterion that makes it possible to distinguish an authentic development from a corruption.

64 Newman, *Development of Christian Doctrine*, p. 325.

65 Ibid.

66 Ibid.

67 Ibid.

68 Newman also mentions other principles: the principle of the spiritual interpretation of Scripture, the principle of grace, the principle of asceticism, the principle of the malignity of sin, and the principle that matter is capable of sanctification, adding that others could be listed. Ibid., pp. 325–326.

69 Ibid., p. 354.

A third criterion of discernment is "power of assimilation".[70] A healthy organism can take in food, water, oxygen, etc., transforming all this into vital force. In the same way, living ideas have the power to penetrate the real, to assimilate other ideas, to stimulate thought, and to develop without losing their own identity and inner unity. Because of the dogmatic principle, Christianity has been able to incorporate various theological arguments, philosophical thoughts, and linguistic expressions into its doctrine, while discarding erroneous aspects. This has occurred in complex historical processes of conflict, purification, clarification, and incorporation. An example of this is the non-biblical term *ὁμοούσιον τῷ πατρί* (*homoùsion to Patri:* of the same substance as the Father), inserted by the Council of Nicaea (325) into the heart of the Creed to express in a clear way, against the Arian heresy, the divinity of the Son of God made man. Newman sees a similar process of assimilation in the area of the sacraments and sacramentals: "The use of temples, and these dedicated to particular saints, and ornamented on occasions with branches of trees; incense, lamps, and candles; votive offerings on recovery from illness; holy water; asylums; holydays and seasons, use of calendars, processions, blessings on the fields; sacerdotal vestments, the tonsure, the ring in marriage, turning to the East, images at a later date, perhaps the ecclesiastical chant, and the Kyrie Eleison, are all of pagan origin, and sanctified by their adoption into the Church."[71] Such forms of assimilation are not signs of decadence or infidelity to the origins but of the integration of the true, the

70 Ibid., chap. V, sec. III.

71 Ibid., p. 373. It appears that Newman does not always distinguish between derivations from practices widespread in paganism and customs known among the people of Israel, but the general principle seems correct: many signs that Christians use to sanctify their lives come from other traditions or customs and, having been purified from pagan beliefs and then incorporated into the practice of the Church, constitute signs of blessing and grace.

sacred, and the good that is found everywhere, also constituting a test of the strength of the dogmatic and sacramental principles. On the other hand, if certain extraneous elements tend to enter Christianity but cannot be assimilated and are not expelled there is a danger of corruption.

"Logical sequence"[72] can be listed as the fourth criterion of discernment. According to Newman, the development of doctrine is a vital process too comprehensive to be understood only as a logical deduction starting from certain premises.[73] But he reiterates that the different doctrines must be logically consistent with the initial data and with each other, constituting an inner connection that can be recognised *a posteriori*. As an example of this criterion Newman describes the logical coherence existing between the sacrament of baptism, the penitential discipline of the first centuries, and the doctrine of purgatory. In the post-apostolic period a controversy arose over the possibility of reconciliation for Christians who had received the sacrament of baptism for the forgiveness of sins but had fallen into grave sin. Quite early on, with reference to some of the Lord's words, various forms of penitential discipline arose in the Church, regulated by the authority of the bishop. Since it was not ruled out that a repentant sinner might die without having completed his penitential journey, the question then arose as to the fate of such a believer. As a result, also on the basis of various indications from Scripture and the practice of praying for the deceased, the doctrine of purgatory developed. Newman spots a logical coherence between baptism for the forgiveness of sins, the discipline of penance, and the doctrine of purgatory. A similar logic, according to him, characterises every authentic development.

72 Ibid., chap. V, sec. IV.

73 According to Newman, the development of Christian doctrine cannot be understood only as "a conscious reasoning from premises to conclusion" (Ibid., p. 189). He always opposed a purely intellectualistic conception of doctrinal development.

A development can therefore be judged by its consequences and recognised as true or false based on its fruits.

A fifth criterion for discerning a legitimate development is "anticipation of its future".[74] Given that the different doctrines form a unified body and are coherently connected to one another, it can be assumed that tendencies that only come to full fruition later are already discernible, albeit in isolated form, in their earlier history. Such anticipations are signs of the harmony of later developments with earlier ones and with the original idea. In this context Newman mentions the principle that matter, like spirit, is capable of sanctification: the Son of God took on flesh, died in the flesh, and through his resurrection and ascension the flesh is already glorified in the mystery of God. In this principle Newman sees the doctrine of the resurrection of the dead anticipated, but also the dignity of the bodies of the deceased, which Christians treated with respect from the beginning, and the sanctity of the relics of the martyrs, the early object of special veneration. In a similar way, for many doctrines that developed in later times brief allusions and sporadic indications are found in the first ages of the Church, although these are generally recognisable as anticipations only through the subsequent developments.

To this fifth criterion for authentic development corresponds the sixth, that is, "conservative action upon its past".[75] A development is authentic when it preserves and safeguards previous developments. If a development contradicts the central idea or previous dogmatic definitions it is a corruption. Also in this context one can refer, in an analogous way, to the development of the human being: in the physical structure of an adult there is something new, but what was essential in childhood and adolescence is preserved. As an example of this criterion Newman again mentions Marian devotion. He

74 Ibid., chap. V, sec. V.
75 Ibid, chap. V, sec. VI.

emphasises that the Council of Ephesus solemnly declared the title of Mary as Mother of God "to protect the doctrine of the Incarnation, and to preserve the faith of Catholics from a specious Humanitarianism".[76] To this theological argument Newman also adds an empirical observation: the Christian communities that venerate the holy Virgin continue to adore Jesus Christ, while those who reject this devotion often tend to abandon the worship of the Lord as well. For Newman it is clear that authentic developments make new aspects of the original Revelation explicit but cannot be in conflict with previous dogmatic definitions; they must instead illuminate, corroborate, and safeguard them.[77] Every authentic development must be homogeneous.

As the seventh and final criterion for discerning true development Newman mentions "chronic vigour".[78] This criterion means that while a corruption is generally brief, or, if it persists, leads to a process of decadence and disintegration, a faithful development is instead distinguished by its enduring vital force. In history Newman finds many examples that amaze him because they show how the Church has prevailed with its doctrine despite many conflicts with heresies, how it has been able to assert itself against the powers of this world, how it has integrated new elements into its patrimony while remaining faithful to its tradition, and how it has always renewed itself, sometimes after times of profound crisis. Newman also knows the weaknesses and sins of the members of the Church, which sometimes disfigure its human face, and he does not remain silent about the times in which the Church "has been thrown into what was almost a state of *deliquium*",[79] that is, of

76 Ibid., p. 424.

77 Newman does not specify in detail which doctrines are definitive. But taking into account the dogmatic principle, which he always emphasised, he would share the opinion that doctrines proposed by the Church's magisterium as definitive should be considered so.

78 Newman, *Development of Christian Doctrine*, chap. V, sec. VII.

79 Ibid., p. 442.

disintegration. But, after some time, God has granted his Church new strength and vitality: "Her wonderful revivals, while the world was triumphing over her, is a further evidence of the absence of corruption in the system of doctrine and worship into which she has developed. [...] She pauses in her course, and almost suspends her functions; she rises again, and she is herself once more; all things are in their place and ready for action. Doctrine is where it was, and usage, and precedence, and principle, and policy."[80] Such permanent or renewed vitality, sometimes after certain "pauses" in which the Church has not performed its functions with due dedication, is – for Newman – an eloquent sign that in the final analysis it is guided by the Lord himself.

In presenting the last criteria of discernment Newman's explanations become increasingly brief and concise. The exposition of the seventh criterion fills only seven pages. As he writes these lines, in fact, he already knows in conscience where his path will lead him. He always follows the maxim: "Truth is not known by being told, but by being done."[81] Newman's essay ends abruptly with the following words: "There may be changes, but they are consolidations or adaptations; all is unequivocal and determinate, with an identity which there is no disputing. Indeed it is one of the most popular charges against the Catholic Church at this very time, that she is 'incorrigible': – change she cannot [in her substantial identity], if we listen to St. Athanasius or St. Leo; change she never will, if we believe the controversialist or alarmist of the present day."[82] Amid all the changes and developments discoverable in the history

80 Ibid.

81 Biemer, *Die Wahrheit wird stärker sein*, p. 200.

82 Newman, *Development of Christian Doctrine*, p. 442. Here Newman uses the typical language of those who, after a long search, have finally found the haven of the Church, and expresses his amazement and gratitude to the Lord, who through his Spirit continually reinvigorates the Church. He again uses some important terms, for example, "substantial identity" or "an identity which there is no disputing," without describing them more precisely, in part because he has already decided to convert and to conclude his essay.

of Catholic doctrine, Newman thus finds a "substantial identity", a dynamic centre of truth that does not change and becomes ever clearer in the course of the centuries. Although Newman's terminology is in part imprecise, his insights are fascinating, his explanations illuminating, and his numerous examples easy to understand.

The essential outlines of the second part of the essay can be summarised in this way: Newman intends to show how, on the basis of seven criteria, it is possible to distinguish authentic developments of Christian doctrine from its alterations and corruptions. The starting point is (1) the *preservation of type*, that is, of the general physiognomy of the Church, which is supernatural, catholic and Roman. Every faithful development is then distinguished (2) by the *continuity of the principles* underlying it, especially those of dogma, faith, theology, and the sacramental order. Because of the strength of these principles the Church therefore possesses (3) a notable *power of assimilation* of new ideas and customs, without losing its identity of doctrine, life, and worship. The connection with the origins and with previous doctrines cannot be arbitrary but must show (4) a *logical sequence*, generally detectable *a posteriori*. Because of this inner connection, one can find for subsequent developments (5) *germinal anticipations* in previous phases. At the same time, any authentic new developments make new aspects of the original Revelation explicit, but are characterised (6) by *conservative action upon the past*, in that they safeguard previous dogmatic developments and definitions. In this process of development, finally, Catholic doctrine possesses (7) a *chronic vigour*, which cannot come from the often weak members of the Church but only from God himself, who continues to guide his people on the journey.

Newman thus demonstrates that the development of Christian doctrine is not arbitrary, even if it can never be predicted in advance. This development follows certain criteria that can be recognised and verified; it proceeds in a homogeneous way and leads in a precise direction; it generally leads to greater clarity; it goes through changes and discontinuities in matters pertaining or connected to time but moves within a "substantial identity". All the members of the Church, in different ways, participate in this development. Yet it is the Spirit of God who leads the Church into all truth (cf. *John* 16:13).[83]

3. Permanent relevance

With his essay on the development of Christian doctrine Newman addressed a question that at his time was rather new and little-explored. Some aspects of his theory were further specified and expanded in the 20th century by theologians like Henri de Lubac,[84] Karl Rahner[85] and Yves Congar.[86] Newman's reflections, however, are still of considerable relevance and can shed light on some of the challenges of our time, for example, on the correct interpretation of Vatican Council II and the debates regarding the future path of the Church.

In his address to the Roman curia on 22 December 2005, Benedict XVI spoke of the reception of Vatican Council II forty years after its conclusion.[87] He first mentioned a false interpretation of

83 In his book *Il dogma in divenire* Seewald offers a great deal of interesting information on the problem of the development of dogma in the course of history. He also summarises Newman's thinking, but criticises it as "essayistic" because it presents many things that "appear plausible, but are not explained more rigorously" (p. 170). This criticism, which has some basis in Newman's sometimes imprecise terminology, does not seem to do justice to Newman's profound theological reflections. Seewald himself describes the problem of the development of dogma as the Church's ongoing effort to translate the Gospel message in a way plausible for the believers of every time, as "the unstable simultaneity of continuity and discontinuity" (p. 240). Compared with this rather formal definition, Newman's criteria seem more lively, concrete, and meaningful.

84 H. de Lubac, *Il problema dello sviluppo del dogma*, in *Mistica e mistero cristiano* (Opera Omnia 6) (Jaca Book: 2018), pp. 227–257.

85 K. Rahner, *Sul problema dell'evoluzione del dogma*, in *Saggi teologici* (Paoline: 1965), pp. 261–325.

86 Y. Congar, *Progresso della Chiesa nell'intelligenza della fede*, in *La Fede e la Teologia*, (Desclée: 1967), pp. 103–131.

87 Cf. Benedict XVI, Address to the Roman curia, offering them his Christmas greetings, 22 December 2005. This address sparked a broad debate among theologians that

the council, calling this the 'hermeneutic of discontinuity', which risks ending up in a rupture between the pre-conciliar Church and the post-conciliar Church. Put simply, today this hermeneutic has essentially two expressions.

On the one hand there are groups according to which the Church must move beyond the texts of the council and take on a form altogether different from before, finally adapting to the demands of modernity. For this reason it must reject certain doctrines considered no longer plausible by the vast majority of people and therefore untenable, as, for example, that the Church as the people of God has a constitutionally hierarchical structure, that marriage is a union between a man and a woman, and that the priesthood is reserved only for men.[88] These groups are in danger of confusing the concept of "development" with that of "alteration" or "adaptation" to the spirit of the times.

On the other hand there are groups that reject some of the council's teachings, for example, those regarding religious freedom, ecumenism, dialogue with other religions, and liturgical renewal.[89]

continues today. Among the numerous publications on the topic, cf. above all, R. Weimann, *Dogma und Fortschritt bei Joseph Ratzinger* (Schöningh: 2012). Pope Francis confirmed the relevance of Benedict XVI's theological thought, stating that "his thinking and insights continue to be fruitful and effective. Recently we commemorated the sixtieth anniversary of the opening of the Second Vatican Council. As we know, Benedict XVI personally participated as an expert and played an important role in the genesis of some of its documents. Afterwards, he was called to guide the ecclesial community in its implementation, both at the side of St John Paul II and then as Pastor of the universal Church. Pope Benedict helped us to interpret the conciliar documents in depth by proposing a 'hermeneutic of reform and continuity'. Even most recently, he sought to stress how the Council continues to exercise its crucial function, since it provides us with the necessary guidelines for reformulating the central question of the nature and mission of the Church in our time." Francis, Address for the conferral of the "Ratzinger Prize", 1 December 2022.

88 These examples are not mentioned by Benedict XVI and are rather random and arbitrary. Other doctrines contested by certain groups, but definitively taught by the Church, could also be mentioned.

89 It appears that these four elements of conciliar doctrine are the central points contested by the Priestly Fraternity of St Pius X.

According to them, such teachings are contrary to Tradition and therefore erroneous. Groups of this sort tend to oppose development as such.

The one see the true Church in a new post-conciliar form, which definitively breaks with the pre-conciliar Church and some of its doctrines. The other find the true Church in the pre-conciliar form, maintaining that the council constitutes a rupture and that the post-conciliar Church is no longer in the full truth. Both groups advocate a hermeneutic of discontinuity, which conflicts with a sound understanding of "development".

The hermeneutic of discontinuity is opposed by "the 'hermeneutic of reform', of renewal in the continuity of the one subject-Church which the Lord has given to us. She is a subject which increases in time and develops, yet always remaining the same, the one subject of the journeying People of God."[90] The hermeneutic of discontinuity, therefore, is not overcome by promoting a simple hermeneutic of continuity, which would exclude any type of growth, renewal, and development. To correctly understand the conciliar texts, and also the other documents of the Church's magisterium, one must apply a hermeneutic of reform, but of reform in continuity. In this process of reform there may be elements of "discontinuity": these, however, do not concern the fundamental decisions of the Church, for example, dogmatic clarifications and definitive statements, but rather their applications and concretisations in a certain historical period.[91] Every true renewal is therefore connected with developments that can entail changes and

90 Benedict XVI, Address to the Roman curia, offering them his Christmas greetings, 22 December 2005.

91 It seems difficult to decide *a priori* which elements of a doctrine can change, because they are tied to their historical and contingent expression, and which belong to their irreformable substance. Certainly, dogmatic definitions and definitive doctrines cannot change. In this regard it is necessary to examine each individual case of development, evaluating the various aspects at play and seeking to feel, think, and walk with the Church.

make new aspects of Revelation explicit, but without altering the Church in its substance and its defined faith.

Newman's reflections on the development of Christian doctrine can contribute to the overcoming of extreme positions in the treatment of these important questions, fostering the path of authentic renewal.

To those who look with suspicion on possible developments of Christian doctrine, Newman would recall that such developments are presumable from the very beginning, because Christian Revelation is never completely exhausted and must be impressed upon the faithful of all places and all times. Moreover, two millennia of Church history testify to the fact that there have been numerous doctrinal developments over time, often in confrontation with errors and heresies, leading the Church to greater clarity in its doctrine. Finally, it must not be forgotten that authentic developments of the ecclesial organism are signs of life. One who rejects such developments on principle turns the Church into a museum of the past and a dead organism.

To those who reject certain doctrines deemed no longer plausible for the modern person, seeking to adapt the Church to the demands of this world, Newman would say that genuine developments of doctrine have nothing to do with their alteration or corruption. The Church has always gone against the tide, urging the faithful not to conform to this world, but to be transformed by the renewal of their way of thinking, in order to be able to discern God's will (cf. *Rom* 12:2). As the Oxford theologian emphasises at the end of his essay, in all the changes and developments there is a substantial identity. The Church cannot change its identity: it is called to remain faithful to the Lord and his Revelation, while continuing its historical journey towards definitive fulfilment.

The seven criteria that Newman elaborates can also be helpful in various current debates, for discerning between authentic developments in doctrine and their deviations and falsifications, offering useful indications for the path to take. They are so timely that a 1990 document by the International Theological Commission entitled *The Interpretation of Dogma* presents them in full in its discussion of the problem of the development of dogmas.[92] Presented below are some brief examples aimed at proposing their implementation.

- When certain currents of thought tend to adapt Christian doctrine to the spirit of the world, to promote nationalistic aspirations, or to disregard the papal magisterium, they contradict the general physiognomy of the ecclesial type, which, according to Newman, is supernatural, catholic, and Roman. Authentic progress in the understanding of Revelation can only take place in accord with the Catholic faith professed, lived, and celebrated by the universal Church, of which the college of bishops, in communion with the successor of Peter, is the ultimate guarantor (first criterion).[93]
- Authentic developments take into account the dogmatic principle according to which faith is a question of truth. They respect the principle of theology, which rejects irrational and sentimental tendencies, and respond to the sacramental principle, which values the signs of the sacraments as efficacious means of grace and protects them from inappropriate flattening, above all the Eucharist, the "source" and "summit" of the whole life of the Church (second criterion).[94]
- If these principles are taken into account, all that is true, sacred, and good in the world, through a process of evaluation, purification, and integration, can be assimilated into the doctrine of the Church. But if genuine faith is distorted or obscured by

92 Cf. International Theological Commission, *The Interpretation of Dogma*, 1990, 3, 3, 5: "The Seven Criteria of J.H. Newman".

93 Cf. Vatican Council II, Dogmatic constitution on divine revelation *Dei Verbum*, nos. 8 and 10.

94 Cf. Vatican Council II, Constitution on the sacred liturgy *Sacrosanctum Concilium*, no. 10.

foreign and unassimilable elements, for example by syncretistic forms of prayer, this is a corruption (third criterion).[95]

- New doctrines are authentic when they demonstrate an inner connection with other Christian doctrines and a "logical" consistency with the faith. This can certainly be said of the theology of the body proposed by John Paul II.[96] Such consistency, however, is not seen in the demands for a change in sexual morality, such as that for the moral approval of sexual acts between persons of the same sex (fourth criterion).[97]
- If anticipations of new developments are found in earlier times, this is a criterion of their authenticity. This could be applied, for example, to the doctrine of the "seeds of the Word" (St Justin, etc.) sown everywhere as germs of truth. This doctrine presents a certain anticipation of a sound "theology of religions" that recognises what is good and true in different religions and interprets this as a preparation for the Gospel (fifth criterion).[98]
- Authentic developments do not obscure the central idea of Christianity or previously defined doctrinal truths, but protect and safeguard them. In this sense the personalist teaching of marriage as a covenant can be called an authentic development: it enhances the view of marriage in the light of salvation history, presenting it as an image of the covenant between Christ and the Church, while at the same time preserving its previous understanding as a contract between a man and a woman.[99]

95 Cf. Congregation for the Doctrine of the Faith, Letter on some aspects of Christian meditation *Orationis Formas*, 15 October 1989, no. 12.

96 Cf. John Paul II, Catecheses at the Wednesday general audiences, 1979–1984; Francis, Post-synodal apostolic exhortation on love in the family *Amoris Laetitia*, 19 March 2016, no. 151.

97 Cf. Congregation for the Doctrine of the Faith, Letter on the pastoral care of homosexual persons *Homosexualitatis Problema*, 1 October 1986.

98 Cf. International Theological Commission, *Christianity and the World Religions*, 1996, nos. 41–45; Vatican Council II, Dogmatic constitution on the Church *Lumen Gentium*, no. 16.

99 Cf. Vatican Council II, Pastoral constitution on the Church in the contemporary world *Gaudium et Spes*, no. 48.

Certain changes called for in some places, however, that break with definitive doctrines – for example, regarding the sacramental and hierarchical structure of the Church[100] or the reservation of the priestly ministry to men alone – would not be legitimate developments (sixth criterion).[101]

- True developments do not create confusion but bring new vitality: Pope Francis's decisive "no" to the death penalty, in the footsteps of his predecessors, is an example of such an authentic development. The new revision of the respective number 2267 of the *Catechism of the Catholic Church* brings greater clarity to an aspect of the Gospel, that is, that even a criminal does not lose their personal dignity. Preserved at the same time, indeed clarified and strengthened, is the traditional principle that every human life, from conception to natural death, must be protected (seventh criterion).[102]

These few examples show that Newman's seven criteria have enduring relevance for the theology and life of the Church. Still today they can help in distinguishing between authentic developments that are in accord with Catholic identity and obfuscations, distortions, and false adaptations to the spirit of the times.

[100] Cf. Vatican Council II., Dogmatic constitution on the Church *Lumen Gentium*, nos. 18–29.

[101] Cf. John Paul II, Letter on reserving priestly ordination to men alone *Ordinatio Sacerdotalis*, 22 May 1994.

[102] Cf. Congregation for the Doctrine of the Faith, New revision of number 2267 of the *Catechism of the Catholic Church* on the death penalty – rescriptum "Ex audentia ss.mi", 1 August 2018.

III. The Transmission of Sound Doctrine: The Testimony of the Faithful

Pope Francis often dreamed of a Church in which all the baptised would collaborate in its mission. On 17 October 2015 – fifty years after Paul VI established the Synod of Bishops – he gave an address in which he presented his ideas on such a Church. After a brief overview of the course of the Synod of Bishops in the past, he stated: "We must continue along this path. The world in which we live, and which we are called to love and serve, even with its contradictions, demands that the Church strengthen co-operation in all areas of her mission. It is precisely this path of synodality which God expects of the Church of the third millennium. What the Lord is asking of us is already in some sense present in the very word 'synod'. Journeying together – laity, pastors, the Bishop of Rome – is an easy concept to put into words, but not so easy to put into practice."[103]

The commitment to such a form of Church-communion, therefore, implies not only a deepened collaboration of the bishops with the successor of Peter but also a greater involvement of all the faithful who, as baptised and confirmed, are full-fledged members of the people of God, thus also participating in its mission. All members of the Church are endowed with the Holy Spirit so that they may shine as lights in the world, living and transmitting the treasury of sound doctrine.

103 Francis, Address for the ceremony commemorating the 50th anniversary of the institution of the Synod of Bishops, 17 October 2015.

Addressing this same theme, John Henry Newman wrote a famous essay entitled *On Consulting the Faithful in Matters of Doctrine.*[104] This work sparked bitter disputes right from its publication. A good understanding of its significance requires first of all a description of the context in which it was born.

1. *The context*

Newman's study was published in 1859 in *The Rambler*, an important magazine for educated Catholics in England at the time. Founded in 1848, the periodical was esteemed by many laypeople, while some bishops viewed it with concern. Their reservations were dictated in part by personal reasons, but also by various articles in which the well-known editor-in-chief, Richard Simpson, a converted former Anglican minister, had openly and at times in a polemical tone denounced various defects and weaknesses of the Catholic Church.

At the beginning of 1859 the situation became critical. The English government established a Royal Commission on Elementary Education, which was meant to support Catholic schools as well. But Catholics did not assert their right to collaborate with the commission, since the bishops had decided not to engage in such collaboration, as the commission also intended to examine methods of religious instruction. The January edition of the *Rambler* published an article on the matter, written by Scott Nasmyth Stokes, inspector of Catholic schools, in which he respectfully but clearly rejected the arguments presented against collaboration with the royal commission. This article was interpreted as an expression of disloyalty to the episcopate. Subsequently, in order to avoid a public scandal, Cardinal Nicholas Wiseman, archbishop

104 Valuable for a correct understanding of the essay is the long and detailed Introduction by John Coulson, in J.H. Newman, *On Consulting the Faithful in Matters of Doctrine* (Sheed & Ward: 1961), pp. 1–49.

of Westminster, and William Ullathorne, bishop of Birmingham, asked Simpson to resign and Newman take over as editor of the *Rambler*. Not without concern, Newman gave his consent so as to save the important periodical and contribute to keeping peace in the Church.

Newman decided to change the magazine's tone but not its basic outlook. At first his approach was to the liking of the bishops and also of Sir John Acton, the magazine's well-known owner. In the May 1859 edition Newman sought to clarify the *Rambler's* position on the sensitive issue of the royal commission. To this end he published extensive excerpts from the pastoral letters of Cardinal Wiseman and Bishop Ullathorne, while adding that on the question of elementary education it would be helpful for prelates to know the opinion of the laity: "*If even in the preparation of a dogmatic definition the faithful are consulted*, as lately in the instance of the Immaculate Conception, it is at least as natural to anticipate such an act of kind feeling and sympathy in great practical questions [...]."[105] (Emphasis is Coulson's.)

Because of this sentence, theology professor John Gillow accused Newman of heresy. Immediately rejecting the accusation, Newman asked his bishop, Ullathorne, for a theological censor for the *Rambler*, in order to have the matter clarified objectively by an expert. But the bishop, not considering such a measure appropriate, visited Newman and asked him to shut down the *Rambler*. He was not able to understand why the formation of the laity could be important for the Church, and considered the May issue of the *Rambler* inappropriate: "There were remains of the old spirit. It was irritating. Our laity were a peaceable set [...]. They had a deep faith; they did not like to hear that anyone doubted."[106] Newman's note about the meeting continues: "I stated my own view strongly [...];

105 Ibid., "Introduction", p. 8.
106 Ibid., p. 18.

he saw only one side, I another [...]. He said something like 'Who are the laity?' I answered (not these words) that the Church would look foolish without them."[107] Although Newman could not understand the bishop's attitude he accepted his request without hesitation. Afterward he wrote to a friend: "I then promised him I would give up the *Rambler* after the July Number. There was no sort of unpleasantness of any kind in our conversation from beginning to end. It is impossible, with the principles and feelings on which I have acted all through life, that I could have acted otherwise. I never have resisted, nor can resist, the voice of a lawful Superior, speaking in his own province."[108]

With this decision, however, the case was not closed. Newman had yet to publish the July issue of the *Rambler*, and he intended to explain more fully the importance of the role of the lay faithful in the Church and the significance of the *sensus fidei*. He maintained, in fact, that this reality was important for the life of the Church. So he published the study *On Consulting the Faithful in Matters of Doctrine*, offering a series of theological and historical arguments in support of his position.

Although no one was able to refute Newman's arguments, serious objections were soon raised against him. Professor Gillow even accused him of denying the doctrine of the Church's infallibility. Thomas Brown, bishop of Newport, translated some passages of the article into Latin, making a few mistakes, and reported it to the Congregation for the Propagation of the Faith, at the time still responsible for ecclesial matters in England. Newman, informed of the reservations regarding his article, in January 1860 wrote to Cardinal Wiseman, who was in Rome, asking him for a list of the incriminated passages and a precise indication of the dogmatic pronouncements they were held to have violated, also stating his

107 Ibid., pp. 18–19.

108 Newman, *Letters and Diaries*, vol. XIX (Clarendon Press: 1961), p. 150.

readiness to reformulate his arguments in full accord with those pronouncements. Newman's letter was forwarded to *Propaganda Fide*, which compiled a list of the statements against which objections had been raised, asking Newman to provide the necessary clarifications. This list, however, was never sent to Newman. He received only, months later, a letter informing him that Cardinal Wiseman had resolved the question in an acceptable manner. In reality nothing had been resolved: Cardinal Alessandro Barnabò, prefect of *Propaganda Fide*, deemed Newman disobedient because he had not offered any response. Newman did not know anything specific about the objections raised against him, and so could not justify himself. Among the radical ultramontanists Newman was considered a dangerous man. Monsignor George Talbot, an English convert working in Rome as prelate of the Antechamber of the Apostolic Palace, wrote to Archbishop Henry Manning: "It is perfectly *true* that a cloud has been hanging over Dr Newman" since he wrote the *Rambler* article, and "none of his writings since have removed that cloud."[109] Regarding the laity, Talbot went on to say that "they are beginning to show the cloven hoof [...]. They are only putting into practice the doctrine taught by Dr Newman in his article in the *Rambler* [...]. What is the province of the laity? To hunt, to shoot, to entertain. These matters they understand, but to meddle with ecclesiastical matters they have no right at all [...]. Dr Newman is the most dangerous man in England."[110]

For several years a shadow of distrust surrounded Newman, who for his part did not publish any writings. Only in 1864, when in the *Apologia Pro Vita Sua* he began to illustrate the development of his thought and his journey towards the haven of the Catholic Church, did the accusations against him prove to be without any foundation. In 1867 the misunderstandings were definitively cleared up

109 Newman, "Introduction", *On Consulting the Faithful*, p. 41.
110 Ibid., pp. 41–42.

with *Propaganda Fide*, when two Birmingham Oratorians heard, during a visit to Rome, that Newman stood accused of not having responded to the list of incriminating statements. The two pointed out that Newman had never received such a list. Subsequently Pope Pius IX himself, informed of the matter, asked Paul Cullen, archbishop of Dublin, to comment on Newman's orthodoxy. After a positive report from the Irish prelate, it became clear to all that the objections against Newman had in reality been mere slander.

During this period of suffering Newman wrote to his friend Henry Wilberforce: "If you attempt at a wrong time, what in itself is right, you perhaps become a heretic or schismatic. What I may aim at may be real and good, but it may be God's will it should be done a hundred years later. [...] When I am gone, it will be seen perhaps that persons stopped me from doing a work which I might have done. God overrules all things. Of course it is discouraging to be out of joint with the time, and to be snubbed and stopped as soon as I begin to act."[111] Newman was a forerunner of later times. His thoughts – including those on the mission of the lay faithful and the *consensus fidelium* – were fully embraced by the Church a hundred years later and still remain stimulating and fruitful.

2. The content

Newman, basing himself on various patristic studies, starts from the fact that the apostolic Tradition is entrusted to the whole Church and that all the components of the ecclesial body have a specific responsibility for its custody and transmission. Tradition is manifested differently depending on the times: "sometimes by the mouth of the episcopacy, sometimes by the doctors, sometimes by the people, sometimes by liturgies, rites, ceremonies, and customs, by events, disputes, movements, and all those other

[111] Newman, *Letters and Diaries*, vol. XIX (Clarendon Press: 1961), pp. 179–180.

phenomena which are comprised under the name of history".[112] From this fact Newman concludes that "none of these channels of tradition may be treated with disrespect", adding right away, however, that "the gift of discerning, discriminating, defining, promulgating, and enforcing any portion of that tradition resides solely in the *Ecclesia docens*".[113] Every believer is free to underscore, with greater emphasis, one or another aspect of this reality. Newman then writes, "for myself, I am accustomed to lay great stress on the *consensus fidelium*".[114]

2.1 This view helped Newman resolve some difficulties in regard to the development of Christian doctrine. The Tradition of the Church, in fact, is not to be understood as a mechanical transmission of the contents of the faith, but as a process of an organism that lives and grows. This process is objectively verifiable through historical testimonies. But Tradition also has a subjective meaning: all the members of the Church, by virtue of the gift of the Spirit, are its bearers. Why, then, is it necessary to value the consensus of the faithful? "Because the body of the faithful is one of the witnesses to the fact of the tradition of revealed doctrine, and because their *consensus* through Christendom is the voice of the Infallible Church".[115] The consensus of the faithful is therefore able to fill in any gaps in the patristic testimonies on individual points of Catholic doctrine.

Newman then refers first of all to Giovanni Perrone, SJ, with whom he had discussed this topic extensively during his stay in Rome in 1847, when, after his conversion (1845), he was preparing for priestly ordination in the Catholic Church. In his work on the Immaculate Conception Perrone speaks of the *sensus Ecclesiae*,

112 Newman, *On Consulting the Faithful*, p. 63.
113 Ibid.
114 Ibid.
115 Ibid.

describing it as a *conspiratio* of the pastors and the faithful. As for the *sensus fidelium*, he maintains that it has a force "distinct (not separate) from the teaching of their pastors".[116] With Gregory of Valencia he affirms: "If on a controversial matter of religion a concordant judgement of all the faithful were to be established [...] the Pontiff could and should rely on this as the judgement of the infallible Church"; such strong words must not be taken "to mean strictly that infallibility is in the 'consensus fidelium,' but that that 'consensus' is an *indicium* or *instrumentum* to us in the judgement of the Church which *is* infallible."[117] (Emphasis is Newman's.) As an example of a definition of the Church's magisterium on the basis of the consensus of the faithful, Fr Perrone mentions the dogma of the beatific vision of souls after purgatory and before the last judgement, a dogma defined by John XXII in the 14th century, not on the basis of specific texts of Scripture or the Fathers but of the unanimous consensus and vigorous sentiments of the faithful.[118]

Newman then refers to the encyclical letter with which Pius IX, preparing the 1854 dogma, asked the bishops to inform him about devotion to the Immaculata on the part of the clergy and the lay faithful, and about their aspiration to have the respective teaching defined as dogma. He cites as well the text of the bull of definition itself, in which the Pontiff, among the various testimonies, also lists the *singularis catholicorum Antistitum ac fidelium conspiratio*, and Newman comments: "The two, the Church teaching and the Church taught, are put together, as one twofold testimony, illustrating each other, and never to be divided."[119]

Finally, Newman also makes mention of his bishop, Ullathorne, who in a treatise published after the proclamation of the dogma

116 Ibid., p. 66.
117 Ibid., p. 67.
118 Cf. ibid., pp. 69–70.
119 Ibid., p. 71.

described the universal conviction of the lay faithful as a *mirror* of the pastors' teaching. Referring to the May edition of the *Rambler*, which was so strongly attacked, Newman writes not without irony: "Well, I suppose a person may *consult* his glass, and in that way may know things about himself which he can learn in no other way."[120] (Emphasis is Newman's.)

2.2 In the next part Newman seeks to explain how the consensus of the faithful relates to the manifestation of the Church's Tradition. With Fr Perrone he maintains that such consensus is a testimony to the apostolic Tradition. When he speaks of *consulting the faithful* he does not mean – as Professor Gillow mistakenly thought – that bishops should seek the advice of the lay faithful or be dependent on their judgement before being able to intervene authoritatively in a matter of doctrine. To *consult* can also mean, especially in spoken English, to verify a matter of fact. "Thus we talk of 'consulting our barometer' about the weather: – the barometer only attests the *fact* of the state of the atmosphere. In like manner, we may consult a watch or a sun-dial about the time of day. A physician consults the pulse of his patient [...]. It is but an index of the state of his health."[121] Only in this sense does Newman mean to speak of consulting the faithful: "Doubtless their advice, their opinion, their judgement on the question of definition is not asked; but the matter of fact, viz. their belief, *is* sought for, as a testimony to that apostolical tradition, on which alone any doctrine whatsoever can be defined."[122] (Emphasis is Newman's.)

The consensus of the faithful, however, is more than a testimony to apostolic Tradition. With Johann Adam Möhler, a well-known exponent of the Tübingen school, Newman also describes it as "a sort of instinct" in the bosom of the mystical body of Christ, which is the

120 Ibid., p. 72.
121 Ibid., p. 54.
122 Ibid., pp. 54–55.

fruit of the communion of believers with God through the sacraments, and forms, so to speak, the conscience of the Church, leading the faithful to spontaneously embrace true doctrine.[123] Referring to Cardinal John Fisher, he then describes it as an impulse from the Holy Spirit, who guides the people of God.[124] With Augustine he also points out that the consensus of the faithful can be understood as an answer to their prayer.[125] For Newman the function of the *consensus fidelium* as the Church's immune system takes on considerable importance: "The religious life of a people is of a certain quality and direction, and these are tested by the mode in which it encounters the various opinions, customs, and institutions which are submitted to it. Drive a stake into a river's bed, and you will at once ascertain which way it is running, and at what speed; throw up even a straw upon the air, and you will see which way the wind blows; submit your heretical and Catholic principle to the action of the multitude, and you will be able to pronounce at once whether it is imbued with Catholic truth or with heretical falsehood."[126]

2.3 To illustrate the relevance of the doctrine of the consensus of the faithful, Newman then speaks extensively of the time of the Arians, to which he had devoted his first great study as an Anglican. That period of the fourth century was "the age of doctors, illustrated, as it was, by the saints Athanasius, Hilary, the two Gregories, Basil, Chrysostom, Ambrose, Jerome, and Augustine, and all of these saints bishops also, except one, nevertheless in that very day the divine tradition committed to the infallible Church was proclaimed and maintained far more by the faithful than by the Episcopate."[127] In making this statement Newman explains that he

123 Cf. ibid., pp. 73–74.
124 Cf. ibid., p. 74.
125 Cf. ibid.
126 Ibid., p. 74–75.
127 Ibid., p. 75.

does not wish to deny that "the great body of the Bishops were in their internal belief orthodox; nor that there were numbers of clergy who stood by the laity, and acted as their centres and guides; nor that the laity actually received their faith, in the first instance, from the Bishops and clergy; nor that some portions of the laity were ignorant, and other portions at length corrupted by the Arian teachers, who got possession of the sees and ordained an heretical clergy."[128] But Newman maintains that "in that time of immense confusion the divine dogma of our Lord's divinity was proclaimed, enforced, maintained, and (humanly speaking) preserved, far more by the 'Ecclesia docta' than by the 'Ecclesia docens'."[129]

Newman confirms his statement with a long list of patristic testimonies. After the Council of Nicaea (325) there was "a temporary suspense of the functions of the *Ecclesia docens*";[130] "the body of the episcopate was unfaithful to its commission";[131]

128 Ibid.

129 Ibid., pp. 75–76. The argument that in the fourth century the doctrine of Christ's divinity was preserved and transmitted more by the lay faithful than by the bishops is controversial among historians. It cannot be exploited to pit pastors against lay faithful. This would be theologically untenable and contrary to Newman's comprehensive vision of the Church. Newman's fundamental intention consists solely in affirming that amid the Arian confusion, sound doctrine was preserved by the ordinary faithful, guided by a few confessor bishops, while many pastors, under the influence of the imperial court establishment, did not exercise their responsibility as teachers of the faith.

130 Ibid., p. 77. This sentence was particularly criticised by Bishop Brown, who considered it contrary to the doctrine of the infallibility of the Church. In 1871 Newman published the third edition of his book *The Arians of the Fourth Century*, adding in the appendix an abridged and revised version of the study *On Consulting the Faithful in Matters of Doctrine*. Newman admitted that he could have expressed himself in a more nuanced way; he honed various parts of the article and added some clarifications to the original text. But he defended himself with the argument that he had not denied the doctrine of the infallibility of the Church, but had only said that there was no authoritative pronouncement of the infallible voice of the Church, in fact, between the Council of Nicaea in 325 and the Council of Constantinople in 381. Cf. Newman, *On Consulting the Faithful*, pp. 112–118.

131 Newman, *On Consulting the Faithful*, p. 76. The expression according to which the "body of Bishops" failed in its confession of the faith was also considered unacceptable. Newman clarified in this regard in 1871 that, in using this term, he had not spoken in a theological but in a historical sense, not in fact thinking of the *corpus episcoporum*, but of the mass of bishops. Cf. ibid., pp. 116–117.

"at one time the Pope, at other times the patriarchal, metropolitan, and other great sees, at other times general councils, said what they should not have said, or did what obscured and compromised revealed truth."[132] Many parts of the Church at that time fell into the heresy of Arianism, above all because numerous bishops, partly under the cruel pressure of the Arian emperors, failed in their duty. The mass of prelates "spoke variously, one against another; there was nothing, after Nicaea, of firm, unvarying, consistent testimony, for nearly sixty years. There were untrustworthy Councils, unfaithful Bishops; there was weakness, fear of consequences, misguidance, delusion, hallucination, endless, hopeless, extending itself into nearly every corner of the Catholic Church. The comparatively few who remained faithful were discredited and driven into exile."[133]

The last of the twenty-two testimonies that Newman presents to demonstrate the negligence of the majority of bishops during that period comes from the pen of Gregory Nazianzen: "If I must speak the truth, I feel disposed to shun every conference of Bishops; for never saw I synod brought to a happy issue, and remedying, and not rather aggravating, existing evils. For rivalry and ambition are stronger than reason, – do not think me extravagant for saying so, – and a mediator is more likely to incur some imputation himself than to clear up the imputations which others lie under."[134]

132 Ibid., p. 76. This phrase, also incriminated, was explained by Newman in the article itself with numerous testimonies, for example, on the weakness of Pope Liberius, who, while remaining orthodox, in exile gave his assent to a condemnation of Athanasius; on the failure of numerous bishops and on the organisation of synods that published professions of faith heretical or ambiguous in character. At the same time he explained in 1871 that by the expression "general councils" he had not meant ecumenical councils but large synods led mostly by Arians. Cf. ibid., pp. 115–118.

133 Ibid., p. 77.

134 Ibid., pp. 85–86.

Newman subsequently lists a series of testimonies that show how "the body of the laity was faithful to its baptism" and was "the ecclesiastical strength of Athanasius, Hilary, Eusebius of Vercellae, and other great solitary confessors, who would have failed without them".[135] Basil, for example, attests: "Matters have come to this pass; *the people have left their houses of prayer*, and assemble in deserts: a pitiable sight; *women and children, old men, and [others] infirm*, wretchedly faring in the open air, amid the most profuse rains and snow-storms, and winds, and frosts of winter; and again in summer under a scorching sun. To this they submit, because they *will have no part in the wicked Arian leaven*."[136] (Emphasis is Newman's.)

Hilary writes to the Emperor Constantius: "Not only in words, but in tears, we beseech you to save the Catholic Churches from any longer continuance of these most grievous injuries, and of their present intolerable persecutions and insults, which moreover they are enduring, which is monstrous, from our brethren. Surely your clemency should listen to the *voice of those who cry out so loudly*, I am a Catholic, I have no wish to be a heretic."[137] (Emphasis is Newman's.)

Twenty-one other similar texts written by Fathers are presented to demonstrate the consensus of the faithful in the major cities of Christendom back then. At a time in which synods and bishops could not affirm the faith in its integrity, the consensus of the faithful was capable of safeguarding and transmitting the dogma of the divinity of the Lord Jesus.

At the end of the article, Newman speaks of his own times, leaving no doubt about the role of the ecclesiastical magisterium on the one hand and of the consensus of the faithful on the other. He maintains that the reality of the fourth century is not that which characterises the whole history of the Church, much less the times

135 Ibid., p. 76.
136 Ibid., p. 95.
137 Ibid., pp. 100–101.

in which he finds himself living. As for his own times, he expresses appreciation for the bishops' commitment to safeguarding the faith: "Never was the Episcopate of Christendom so devoted to the Holy See, so religious, so earnest in the discharge of its special duties, so little disposed to innovate, so superior to the temptation of theological sophistry."[138] Newman is of the view that this explains why the consensus of the faithful, in the minds of many, has lost much of its relevance.

According to his own conviction, however, each component of the Church "has its proper functions, and no portion can safely be neglected. Though the laity be but the reflection or echo of the clergy in matters of faith, yet there is something in the 'pastorum et fidelium *conspiratio*,' which is not in the pastors alone."[139] (Emphasis is Newman's.) Newman concludes the article by recalling the joy of the faithful at the definition of the dogma of Mary, Mother of God, at the Council of Ephesus (431), and reiterates: "The *Ecclesia docens* is more happy when she has such enthusiastic partisans about her as are here represented, than when she cuts off the faithful from the study of her divine doctrines and the sympathy of her divine contemplations, and requires from them a *fides implicita* in her word, which in the educated classes will terminate in indifference, and in the poorer in superstition."[140]

3. Relevance

Newman never fought on behalf of individual expressions and could serenely admit that some terms of his study could have been more precise. What mattered to him were always the insights, ideas, and contents. These still have considerable relevance and can shed light on some issues in current debate.

138 Ibid., p. 103.
139 Ibid., pp. 103–104.
140 Ibid., p. 106.

3.1 Newman highlights that the Church is to be understood as a *communio* with different organs and a common conscience of faith that is shared by all its members, and cannot fall into error. He anticipated the doctrine authoritatively taught by Vatican Council II regarding the Church-communion and the *sensus fidei*: "The entire body of the faithful, anointed as they are by the Holy One (cf. *John* 2:20, 27), cannot err in matters of belief. They manifest this special property by means of the whole peoples' supernatural discernment in matters of faith when 'from the Bishops down to the last of the lay faithful' (Augustine, *De praedestinatione sanctorum* 14, no. 27) they show universal agreement in matters of faith and morals. That discernment in matters of faith is aroused and sustained by the Spirit of truth. It is exercised under the guidance of the sacred teaching authority, in faithful and respectful obedience to which the people of God accepts that which is not just the word of men but truly the word of God (cf. *1 Thess* 2:13). Through it, the people of God adheres unwaveringly to the faith given once and for all to the saints (cf. *Jude* 3), penetrates it more deeply with right thinking, and applies it more fully in its life."[141]

Although Newman still uses the concepts, outmoded in the meantime, of *Ecclesia docens* and *Ecclesia docta,* he is convinced that all the components of the Church have a responsibility for the custody and transmission of the faith. The members of the hierarchy and the lay faithful take on different functions but are called to serve together in Christ's mission in the world. The members of the Church, as the council fathers affirm, "share a true equality with regard to the dignity and to the activity common to all the faithful for the building up of the Body of Christ. For the distinction which the Lord made between sacred ministers and the rest of the People of God bears within it a certain union, since pastors and the other faithful are bound to each other by a mutual need. Pastors of the

[141] Vatican Council II, Dogmatic constitution on the Church *Lumen Gentium*, no. 12.

Church, following the example of the Lord, should minister to one another and to the other faithful. These in their turn should enthusiastically lend their joint assistance to their pastors and teachers. Thus in their diversity all bear witness to the wonderful unity in the Body of Christ. This very diversity of graces, ministries and works gathers the children of God into one, because 'all these things are the work of one and the same Spirit' (*1 Cor* 12:11)."[142]

Newman stands out for having developed a balanced ecclesiology that highlights the specific mission of the various components of the people of God. Starting from the mystery of the Church, he emphasises the necessary unity and collaboration among all its members and is therefore opposed to any ideological opposition between hierarchy, consecrated life and laity. According to him, communion must always be fostered among all members of the people of God, in full respect and recognition of the specific mission of each according to the will of the Lord.

3.2 Newman asks for due appreciation of the consensus of the faithful. In this regard he is not thinking of a sort of magisterial authority from below, but of the significance of faith lived unanimously and with conviction, which, as testimony of faith and charity, is important for the transmission of the Gospel. The conciliar constitution on the Church states in this context: "The holy people of God shares also in Christ's prophetic office; it spreads abroad a living witness to Him, especially by means of a life of faith and charity."[143] The witness of lived faith is, as it were, the echo of the Lord's message, and constitutes a precious support and a source of inspiration for the hierarchy. Newman's request to consider the consensus of the faithful in its true significance "is based on the authority of the testimony of faith in practice, which, according to

142 Ibid., no. 32.

143 Ibid., no. 12.

his conviction, is logically situated within and subordinated to the authority of the Church's magisterium, which represents the sole Teacher of the faith".[144]

In this context Newman repeatedly speaks of the *conspiratio pastorum et fidelium*, which need not mean only a collaboration between pastors and lay faithful, but also mutual encouragement and inspiration. The pressure from some who demand radical changes in Church doctrine from the pastors has nothing to do with the authentic sense of faith of the people of God, but is the expression of a political misunderstanding or worldly view of the Church, which can only lead to confusion and disappointment. In a letter, Newman speaks of the problems that arise "when a number of little Popes start up, laymen often, and preach against Bishops and Priests, and make their own opinions the faith, and frighten simple-minded devout people and drive back inquirers".[145] The consensus of the faithful is not shown in demands of this kind, but in the courageous witness of faith, hope, and charity, in humble service in all areas of life and in authentic fidelity to the Gospel and the Church's doctrine.

3.3 The Pope and the bishops have a particular responsibility for the preservation of the faith. Although Newman primarily emphasises the significance of the *sensus fidei* of the whole people of God, he also frequently mentions the irreplaceable mission of the pastors. He recalls the history of the fourth century, a time of great bishops and doctors, but also of many pastors who, as victims of heresy, compromise, or inertia, did not fulfil their mission.

Newman expresses the hope that such times may never return. But while acknowledging a great difference between the post-Nicene period and that following Vatican II, it does not seem entirely inappropriate to see a certain analogy: just as the first

144 Biemer, *Die Wahrheit wird stärker sein*, p. 309.

145 Newman, *Letters and Diaries*, vol. XXIII (Clarendon Press: 1961), p. 272.

council of the Church, which had clarified the question of Christ's divinity, was followed by a long period of controversies regarding Christological faith, so the era after the last council, during which the doctrine on the Church was enlarged upon and further developed, appears characterised by considerable uncertainty and confusion precisely on ecclesiological questions.

The problems of the fourth century were also caused by the failure of numerous bishops, as Newman emphasises. Regarding the causes of the current crisis of faith, it seems important to avoid unilateral and simplistic responses that do not do justice to the complexity of the situation. But perhaps the fourth century can teach us that mutual support and collaboration between pastors and lay faithful is of vital importance for transmitting the faith to the next generations.

3.4 Of what does the core of the consensus of the faithful consist? Along with other theologians, Newman describes this consensus as testimony to the apostolic Tradition, as a prompting impressed upon the faithful by the Holy Spirit, and as an answer to the prayers of believers. The consensus of the faithful constitutes the fruit and convergent manifestation of the *sensus fidei* of believers. With Möhler, Newman therefore defines the *consensus fidelium* as the common sentiment or conscience of the Church.[146]

Just as the conscience of the individual can spontaneously distinguish between good and evil, so the conscience of the Church enables the people of God to almost instinctively embrace the truth, at the same time rejecting error. A few years before the *Rambler* article Newman had said in his lectures on the Turks: "In that earliest age, it was simply the living spirit of the myriads of the faithful, none of them known to fame, who received from the disciples of our Lord, and husbanded so well, and circulated so widely, and transmitted so faithfully, generation after generation, the once delivered apostolic

[146] Cf. Newman, *On Consulting the Faithful*, p. 73–74.

faith; who held it with such sharpness of outline and explicitness of detail, as enabled even the unlearned instinctively to discriminate between truth and error, spontaneously to reject the very shadow of heresy, and to be proof against the fascination of the most brilliant intellects, when they would lead them out of the narrow way."[147]

This instinctive discernment between truth and error is an expression of the consensus of all the faithful, from the Pope to the ordinary laity, which also embraces those who went before us, and therefore communion with the Church in heaven, with the great saints, the martyrs and confessors, the pastors and doctors, the believers known and unknown who have preserved the apostolic faith intact to the last.

3.5 Today the *sensus fidei* is exposed to many challenges, above all on account of the enormous influence exerted by the mass media, which shape public opinion. Now the *sensus fidei* cannot be assimilated to the public opinion of society. Nor can it be simplistically identified with the majority opinion in the Church. The point of reference that must be kept in view, in fact, is faith and not opinion, which is not rarely the expression of a certain group and a specific tendency, while the *sensus fidei* is the echo of the Gospel.[148]

147 J.H. Newman, *Historical Sketches*, vol. I (Basil Montagu Pickering: 1876), pp. 209–210.

148 Cf. Congregation for the Doctrine of the Faith, Instruction on the ecclesial vocation of the theologian *Donum Veritatis*, 24 May 1990, no. 35: "Actually, the opinions of the faithful cannot be purely and simply identified with the 'sensus fidei'. The sense of the faith is a property of theological faith; and, as God's gift which enables one to adhere personally to the Truth, it cannot err. This personal faith is also the faith of the Church since God has given guardianship of the Word to the Church. Consequently, what the believer believes is what the Church believes. The 'sensus fidei' implies then by its nature a profound agreement of spirit and heart with the Church, 'sentire cum Ecclesia'.

"Although theological faith as such then cannot err, the believer can still have erroneous opinions since all his thoughts do not spring from faith. Not all the ideas which circulate among the People of God are compatible with the faith. This is all the more so given that people can be swayed by a public opinion influenced by modern communications media. Not without reason did the Second Vatican Council emphasise the indissoluble bond between the 'sensus fidei' and the guidance of God's People by

The history of the people of God shows that sometimes it was not the majority but rather a minority who authentically lived the faith. It's enough to think of the *holy remnant* among the people of Israel, or the evangelical movements in the history of the Church, like the Benedictines, the mendicant orders, the Jesuits, or the new spiritual movements and families, which not rarely have begun as small groups regarded with distrust and suspicion. It is therefore very important to distinguish carefully between the *sensus fidei* and majority opinion.

To explore some aspects of this complex topic, a few years ago the International Theological Commission published a document on *Sensus Fidei in the Life of the Church.*[149] This document specifies that from the theological point of view "the *sensus fidei* refers to two realities which are distinct though closely connected, the proper subject of one being the Church, 'pillar and bulwark of the truth' (*1 Tim* 3:15), while the subject of the other is the individual believer, who belongs to the Church through the sacraments of initiation, and who, by means of regular celebration of the Eucharist, in particular, participates in her faith and life. On the one hand the *sensus fidei* refers to the personal capacity of the believer, within the communion of the Church, to discern the truth of faith. On the other hand the *sensus fidei* refers to a communal and ecclesial reality: the instinct of faith of the Church herself, by which she recognises her Lord and proclaims his word. The *sensus fidei* in this sense is reflected in the convergence of the baptised in a lived adhesion to a doctrine of faith or to an element of Christian praxis. This convergence (consensus) plays a vital role in the Church: the

the magisterium of the Pastors. These two realities cannot be separated. Magisterial interventions serve to guarantee the Church's unity in the truth of the Lord. They aid her to 'abide in the truth' in face of the arbitrary character of changeable opinions and are an expression of obedience to the Word of God."

149 International Theological Commission, Sensus fidei *in the life of the Church* (Libreria Editrice Vaticana: 2014).

consensus fidelium is a sure criterion for determining whether a particular doctrine or practice belongs to the apostolic faith."[150]

Refining the ecclesial awareness of the faithful is one of the great tasks of the Church in our day. Indeed, with Newman, it must be emphasised that the Church can fulfil its mission in the world only if its members are mature in the faith, if their ecclesial awareness is functioning and is not distorted by the spirit of the world. Newman's prediction that not well catechised Christians would fall into indifference or superstition has unfortunately come true in a shocking way: today it is necessary to promote the formation of the faithful at all levels. To this end it is necessary to present anew to believers the dispositions needed to develop an authentic participation in the *sensus fidei*, which helps to keep from confusing it with public opinion or the spirit of the times. In this regard certain fundamental attitudes are of particular importance, like listening to the Word, *sentire cum Ecclesia*, openness to reason, adherence to the magisterium, the desire for holiness, and the pursuit of the edification of the Church.[151]

Today there is a need for a new *conspiratio* of pastors and faithful, so that all may participate in the mission of the Church-communion, carrying out their proper tasks and contributing to the evangelisation of the world through a faith lived with joy and conviction. "I would like", Pope Leo XIV said during the Mass for the inauguration of his Petrine ministry, "that our first great desire be for a united Church, a sign of unity and communion, which becomes a leaven for a reconciled world."[152]

150 Ibid., no. 3.
151 Cf. ibid., nos. 88–104.
152 Leo XIV, Homily at the Holy Mass for the beginning of his pontificate, 18 May 2025.

IV. *Apologia Pro Vita Sua*: The One Fold of Christ

Benedict XVI, after beatifying John Henry Newman on 19 September 2010, asked in his Christmas address that same year: "Why was he beatified? What does he have to say to us?" In response he referred to Newman's three conversions, from which "we must learn [...] because they were steps along a spiritual path that concerns us all". He then mentioned the decisive role of conscience: "The path of Newman's conversions is a path of conscience – not a path of self-asserting subjectivity but, on the contrary, a path of obedience to the truth that was gradually opening up to him."[153]

In the *Apologia Pro Vita Sua* these two fundamental aspects are addressed: Newman describes the journey of his conscience and recounts, with great honesty, how God shaped his faith and his religious convictions through a profound conversion, encounters with various people, and engagement with the signs of the times, turning him into a reformer of the Church of England and then leading him to the haven of the Catholic Church. To better understand this classic text it is necessary to consider the situation that led to its composition.[154]

153 Benedict XVI, Address on the occasion of Christmas greetings to the Roman curia, 20 December 2010.

154 Helpful for a correct understanding of the *Apologia*, in addition to the well-known biographies, are the numerous letters that Newman wrote during the months of the composition and publication of the work: cf. Newman, *Letters and Diaries*, vol. XXI.

1. The origin

By 1864 it seemed that Newman had been completely forgotten. Nearly twenty years had passed since his conversion. Most people in England considered him a traitor and thought of the Catholic Church as corrupt, as having rejected the original faith and bound itself to the cause of the Antichrist. These strong statements were then common prejudices against the Church of Rome, from which England had separated under King Henry VIII, due to his conflict with the Pontiff over the annulment of his marriage. Moreover, many openly doubted Newman's personal integrity, unable to explain to themselves how such an intelligent man could have abandoned the Church of England to join a small group of believers on the fringes of English society, who continued to be despised and belittled, in spite of the policy of emancipation enacted in 1829. In the Catholic Church Newman had found inner peace, but his brilliant ideas and initiatives were not understood: the grandiose plan for a Catholic university in Dublin had turned out to be a failure; his prophetic insights on the testimony of the faithful in matters of doctrine were misinterpreted and even suspected of heresy; the Oratory he founded in Birmingham existed in tension with the one in London and seemed on the verge of closure.

Newman had to accept the fact that his life as a Catholic would not bear good fruit. He wrote this observation in his diary: "O how forlorn and dreary has been my course since I have been a Catholic! Here has been the contrast – as a Protestant, I felt my religion dreary, but not my life – but, as a Catholic, my life dreary, not my religion."[155] Newman was then in one of the most difficult struggles of his life; he suffered greatly from his situation and thought he would soon die. But all that changed in the span of a few months.

155 Newman, *Autobiographical Writings*, p. 254.

Why did Newman write the *Apologia*? What was the stimulus, without which he usually never wrote anything? At that time Charles Kingsley, a well-known novelist and professor of history at Cambridge University, published a review of James Anthony Froude's *History of England* in *MacMillan's Magazine*. In this review he wrote: "Truth, for its own sake, had never been a virtue with the Roman clergy. Father Newman informs us that it need not, and on the whole ought not to be; that cunning is the weapon which heaven has given to the Saints wherewith to withstand the brute male force of the wicked world which marries and is given in marriage. Whether his notion be doctrinally correct or not, it is at least historically so."[156]

Newman responded to Kingsley, asking him in turn to prove this serious assertion. Kingsley cited some passages from one of Newman's sermons, which Newman, however, was able to show had been misinterpreted. Kingsley, while declaring himself ready to accept Newman's clarification, nevertheless was unwilling to retract his statement. Newman then decided to publish the correspondence with Kingsley on the matter, securing complete victory in the debate with him.

But Kingsley did not give up: he published a pamphlet in which he amplified the accusations against Newman. He claimed that Newman could not be trusted, his life had not been sincere: he had led, as an Anglican, a Catholic movement, justifying his behaviour by applying certain "Roman" moral principles according to which everything was permissible if it corresponded to his own point of view. The pamphlet, published on Palm Sunday 1864, was entitled: *What Does Dr Newman Mean?*

For more than twenty years Newman had been exposed to public accusations and slander. He had never responded to the attacks, enduring everything with a spirit of penance. He wrote in

156 Newman, *Apologia*, p. vi.

the *Apologia*: "I left their removal to a future day, when personal feelings would have died out, and documents would see the light, which were as yet buried in closets or scattered through the country."[157] But the accusations levelled against him by Kingsley were of another kind: they were not only against him personally, but against the entire Catholic clergy. For this reason, in conscience, he felt compelled to react immediately and with firmness: "Even if I could have found it consistent with my duty to my own reputation to leave such an elaborate impeachment of my moral nature unanswered, my duty to my Brethren in the Catholic Priesthood, would have forbidden such a course. *They* were involved in the charges which this writer, all along, from the original passage in the Magazine, to the very last paragraph of the Pamphlet, had so confidently, so pertinaciously made. In exculpating myself, it was plain I should be pursuing no mere personal quarrel; – I was offering my humble service to a sacred cause. I was making my protest in behalf of a large body of men of high character, of honest and religious minds, and of sensitive honour, – who had their place and their rights in this world, though they were ministers of the world unseen, and who were insulted by my Accuser [...] not only in my person, but directly and pointedly in their own. Accordingly, I at once set about writing the *Apologia Pro Vita Sua*."[158]

From mid-April to mid-June 1864 Newman worked almost non-stop. Volume XXI of his *Letters and Diaries* contains moving texts that show how much this task absorbed him. He worked "from morning to night", even "during dinner time",[159] often sixteen hours a day. Not only did the need to make rapid progress and the strain of writing, correcting, and editing weigh on him, but he also found himself reliving the inner conflict he had experienced

157 Ibid., p. iv.

158 Ibid., p. ix.

159 Newman, *Letters and Diaries*, vol. XXI (Thomas Nelson and Sons Ltd: 1971), p. 103.

years before, so much so that he admitted in a letter: "I have been constantly in tears."[160] With the help of many documents that he had preserved, the good collaboration of numerous friends, and also thanks to his good memory, in a very short time he managed to reconstruct the detailed history of his religious convictions and to put it down in writing; for eight consecutive weeks, a chapter was published every Thursday in the form of a pamphlet. Afterwards the different parts were collected in a single volume.

The *Apologia* is a unique autobiography, sometimes compared with the *Confessions* of St Augustine. Taking his cue from Kingsley's pamphlet, *What Does Dr Newman Mean?*, the famous convert wrote: "He asks what I *mean*; not about my words, not about my arguments, not about my actions, as his ultimate point, but about that living intelligence, by which I write, and argue, and act. He asks about my Mind and its Beliefs and its sentiments; and he shall be answered."[161] In the *Apologia*, for Newman it is not so much a matter of talking about external events – he recounts almost nothing, in fact, about his family, his activities, his travels, his everyday tasks, etc. – as of describing the development of his religious convictions, "my most private thoughts, I might even say the intercourse between myself and my Maker".[162] Newman reveals the story of his conscience, of his search for truth. Only in this way was he able to unmask the accusation that his life was false and insincere. His only desire was "to tell the truth, and to leave the matter in God's hands".[163]

All at once the *Apologia* made Newman famous again. Countless people all over England read it; it was discussed at table, in clubs, on trains, in pubs, and the work passed from hand to hand; it was

160 Ibid., p. 107.

161 Newman, *Apologia*, p. xviii.

162 Ibid., p. xxi.

163 Newman, *Letters and Diaries*, vol. XXI (Thomas Nelson and Sons Ltd: 1971), p. 103.

recommended in church by both Anglican and Catholic preachers; it was commented on in many newspapers and was soon translated into other languages. For public opinion was clear: Newman had won the dispute with Kingsley. Moreover, the *Apologia* played an essential role in strengthening the Catholic Church in England. Newman not only demonstrated his personal sincerity and obedience to the truth, but also spoke on behalf of all Catholic priests, doing much to reduce prejudice against them. So one can understand why not only the bishop of Birmingham but also 558 priests, about half of the English clergy at the time, thanked Newman personally for the publication of the *Apologia*. From abroad – for example, from the German Catholic conference in Würzburg in 1864 – Newman received written acknowledgements. On the Anglican side too the *Apologia* had a positive reception. Many marvelled that Newman should write with such benevolence about the Church of England, and they renewed their friendliness towards him. Even those who could not understand Newman's conversion expressed deep admiration for his beautiful English and the consistency with which he had followed his path. The *Apologia*, much more than other books, certainly contributed to overcoming many prejudices against the Catholic Church among the English. To those who were sincerely seeking the truth it became clear that there was a guiding thread in Newman's life that linked the various stages of his eventful history: obedience to the truth that had been revealed to him step by step in his conscience.

2. *The guiding thread*

The *Apologia* is a demanding read. Newman does not present a novel of his life, but rather lets the objective sources speak for themselves, setting before the reader's eyes numerous people who influenced and directed his religious convictions and describing the progressive development of his thinking with regard to the challenges facing the Church and society of England in the first half of the 19th century. Those who delve into the five chapters of the *Apologia* can get a view of Newman's deepest motivations. The complexity and drama of this journey of conscience obviously cannot be summarised in a few lines. To be brief, the journey can be presented as the fruit of a conversion in three successive stages.

John Henry Newman grew up in the home of his Anglican parents. His mother familiarised him and his siblings with the Bible; what determined everything, however, was not faith, but sentiment. Therefore Newman later wrote that as a child he "had no formed religious convictions".[164] At fourteen he was already reading authors like Hume and Voltaire, whose ideas appeared evident to him and almost stifled his religious predisposition.

The inner storm resulted in his first conversion: "When I was fifteen, (in the autumn of 1816,) a great change of thought took place in me. I fell under the influences of a definite Creed, and received into my intellect impressions of dogma, which, through God's mercy, have never been effaced or obscured."[165] How did he come to this transformation? Newman's family was in financial difficulty, so during the summer holidays of 1816 John Henry, who had fallen ill, had to remain at boarding school. During those weeks, on the advice of a teacher, he read Thomas Scott's *The Force of Truth*. This book struck him deeply. It led him to discover a personal faith in God and to recognise the transience of earthly things. He found peace in the thought of "two and two only absolute and luminously self evident beings, myself and my Creator".[166] From this first conversion Newman's faith received a solid foundation: "From the age of fifteen, dogma has been the fundamental principle of my religion: I know no other religion; I cannot enter into the idea of any other sort of religion; religion, as a mere senti-

164 Newman, *Apologia*, p. 1.

165 Ibid., p. 4.

166 Ibid.

ment, is to me a dream and a mockery. As well can there be filial love without the fact of a father, as devotion without the fact of a Supreme Being."[167]

After completing his studies at Trinity College, Oxford, Newman was elected a fellow of the famous Oriel College, coming into contact with the leading intellectual figures then teaching at Oxford, who influenced his thinking. He also took the decision to enter the service of the Church of England: in 1824 he was ordained a deacon, and a year later he became an Anglican priest; in 1828 he assumed the prestigious post of vicar of St Mary's, the university church. During those years he freed his personality of certain individualistic traits, feeling ever more the influence of some exponents of High Church Anglicanism.

In 1828 he began systematically reading the Church Fathers, a reading that became decisive for him. In 1832 he published his first major study: *The Arians of the Fourth Century*. But while searching for truth under the guidance of the Fathers he noted with deep concern the growing influence of liberal thought in Oxford and all over England. This drove him to found, together with other Anglican clergymen, the Oxford Movement.

The central conviction of this movement was that England was gradually distancing itself from the faith of the early Church and needed a "second Reformation" to restore the spirit of primitive Christianity. The promoters of the Oxford Movement worked primarily through intense homiletic activity and the publication of easily accessible pamphlets. Together with the dogmatic principle, the movement reaffirmed the ecclesiological-sacramental principle: "There was a visible Church, with sacraments and rites which are the channels of invisible grace."[168] Newman was the driving force of the Oxford Movement. The discovery of the visible Church,

167 Ibid., p. 49.
168 Ibid.

with sacraments that are the means of salvation, was the second fundamental stage in his journey of his conscience.

The third principle of the Oxford Movement was the anti-Roman one, with which it meant to fend off the accusation of "popery". Subsequently, seeking to rediscover the theological foundations of Anglicanism, Newman developed the theory of the *Via Media*. This theory was based on the presupposition that the Protestants had denied some fundamental truths of early Christianity, the Catholics instead had sullied the true faith with various innovative additions not founded on Revelation, while the Anglicans had remained faithful to Tradition precisely in choosing the *Via Media*.

The theory of the *Via Media*, however, soon showed its limitations. Is truth always found in the middle? While studying the heresies of the fourth and fifth centuries, Newman soon realised that Anglicanism was in a position similar to that of the heresy of semi-Arianism. The theory of the *Via Media* collapsed like a house of cards. Newman also had to endure Oxford University's condemnation and the Anglican bishops' rejection of his *Tract 90*: an attempt to explain the Thirty-Nine Articles of the Anglican Creed in a Catholic sense, in order to convince supporters of the Oxford Movement not to convert to the Church of Rome, but to work to "catholicise" the Church of England.

Newman then decided, in 1842, to move with some friends to Littlemore, to bring clarity to his future through prayer, study, and fasting. He was convinced that God would give him the necessary light if only he waited patiently, prayed fervently, and listened attentively to the voice of his conscience. In 1843 he retracted all his accusations against the Church of Rome. He also resigned, with deep regret, from his position as a minister of the Church of England. To find a solution to his intellectual difficulties with the Church of Rome, in 1844 he decided to write *An Essay on the Development of Christian Doctrine*. The result of this study was decisive for his third conversion and further path in life. He clearly recognised, in fact, that the more recent Catholic teachings were not corruptions of the doctrine of the primitive Church but rather organic developments of that doctrine in the course of history.

On 8 October 1845, one day before his conversion to the Catholic Church, he wrote a short letter to his family and closest friends: "I am this night expecting Father Dominic, the Passionist [...]. He is a simple, holy man; and withal gifted with remarkable powers. He does not know of my intention; but I mean to ask of him admission into the One Fold of Christ...."[169]

Newman concludes the *Apologia* with a very interesting chapter on his deeply Catholic convictions. He begins with his belief in the existence of God, which to him seems as evident as his own existence, and at the same time notes with startling clarity the spread of faithlessness in modern society. He describes the course of history, summarising: "The disappointments of life, the defeat of good, the success of evil, physical pain, mental anguish, the prevalence and intensity of sin, the pervading idolatries, the corruptions, the dreary hopeless irreligion, that condition of the whole race, so fearfully yet exactly described in the Apostle's words, 'having no hope and without God in the world' – all this is a vision to dizzy and appal; and inflicts upon the mind the sense of a profound mystery, which is absolutely beyond human solution."[170] According to Newman, humanity finds itself entangled by its roots in that evil which theologians call "original sin" and which, according to him, is "almost as certain as that the world exists, and as the existence of God".[171]

Since God does not want humanity to fall into scepticism – Newman continues – it must be admitted that he founded an

169 Ibid., p. 234–235.
170 Ibid., p. 242.
171 Ibid., p. 243.

institution to which he entrusted the full truth of Revelation and the true remedy for humanity's ills: "And thus I am brought to speak of the Church's infallibility, as a provision, adapted by the mercy of the Creator, to preserve religion in the world, and to restrain that freedom of thought, which of course in itself is one of the greatest of our natural gifts."[172] The Church does not teach "that human nature is irreclaimable [...] but to be extricated, purified, and restored; not, that it is a mere mass of hopeless evil, but that it has the promise upon it of great things, and even now, in its present state of disorder and excess, has a virtue and a praise proper to itself. [...] But in the next place she knows and she preaches that such a restoration [...] must be brought about, not simply through certain outward provisions of preaching and teaching [...] but from an inward spiritual power or grace imparted directly from above, and of which she is the channel. She has it in charge to rescue human nature from its misery, but not simply by restoring it on its own level, but by lifting it up to a higher level than its own."[173] Newman professes, with profound conviction, that he wants to belong to this Church which is infallible in matters of faith and morals and which offers humanity the divine remedy of grace.

Finally, Newman addresses a third fundamental theme: the relationship between faith and science. Having expounded the competence of the ecclesiastical magisterium to safeguard Revelation, he now wants to demonstrate how the doctrine of the Church and free scientific research are closely intertwined: "There are two great principles in action in the history of religion, Authority and Private Judgement [...]. Every exercise of Infallibility is brought out into act by an intense and varied operation of the Reason, both as its ally and as its opponent, and provokes again, when it has done its work, a re-action of Reason against it [...]. Catholic Christendom

172 Ibid., p. 245.
173 Ibid., pp. 247–248.

is no simple exhibition of religious absolutism, but presents a continuous picture of Authority and Private Judgement alternately advancing and retreating as the ebb and flow of the tide."[174] The authority of the Church on the one hand defends reason "from its own suicidal excesses",[175] while on the other it requires the full commitment of reason and of contribution from the various theological schools in the various countries of the world. This is part of the catholicity of the Church, which according to Newman is "not only one of the notes of the Church, but, according to the divine purposes, one of its securities".[176] These statements show with what balance Newman describes the relationship between magisterium and scientific research, without falling into fideistic or rationalistic extremism.

3. Relevance

The *Apologia Pro Vita Sua* describes the inner journey of a 19th-century theologian, but it has a significance still valid today.

Newman begins the *Apologia* with a reference to his first conversion, to faith in the living God. Although this description is brief, it sufficiently shows Newman's inner impulse to seek God, whom he discovered in that experience as the true reality. No one has been able to express the significance of this conversion like Benedict XVI, when in his speech on 20 December 2010 he said: "Until that moment, Newman thought like the average men of his time and indeed like the average men of today, who do not simply exclude the existence of God, but consider it as something uncertain, something with no essential role to play in their lives. What appeared genuinely real to him, as to the men of his and our day, is the empirical matter that can be grasped. This is the 'reality'

174 Ibid., p. 252.
175 Ibid., p. 245.
176 Ibid., p. 269.

according to which one finds one's bearings. The 'real' is what can be grasped, it is the things that can be calculated and taken in one's hand. In his conversion, Newman recognised that it is exactly the other way round: that God and the soul, man's spiritual identity, constitute what is genuinely real, what counts. These are much more real than objects that can be grasped. This conversion was a Copernican revolution. What had previously seemed unreal and secondary was now revealed to be the genuinely decisive element. Where such a conversion takes place, it is not just a person's theory that changes: the fundamental shape of life changes. We are all in constant need of such conversion: then we are on the right path."[177] Newman often repeated that faith in God must be "realised", penetrating its truth, adapting to its meaning so that it may shape concrete life. In recent decades this commitment has been put on a secondary level, with the result that many have abandoned the faith. Newman had foreseen this apostasy. Today he would exhort the faithful to convert to what counts, to open their minds and hearts to God, to give him first place in life, in order to be credible witnesses of his presence.

In his first conversion Newman discovered the truth of a personal God who had spoken to him in the depths of his conscience. The *Apologia* shows how he let himself be guided by the voice of conscience, opening himself to the truth step by step and obeying its imperative. Newman is above all a witness and teacher of conscience in its authentic meaning, which today it is absolutely essential to rediscover. Benedict XVI, in the aforementioned speech, said on this subject: "In modern thinking, the word 'conscience' signifies that for moral and religious questions, it is the subjective dimension, the individual, that constitutes the final authority for decision. The world is divided into the realms of the objective and

177 Benedict XVI, Address on the occasion of Christmas greetings to the Roman curia, 20 December 2010.

the subjective. To the objective realm belong things that can be calculated and verified by experiment. Religion and morals fall outside the scope of these methods and are therefore considered to lie within the subjective realm. Here, it is said, there are in the final analysis no objective criteria. The ultimate instance that can decide here is therefore the subject alone, and precisely this is what the word 'conscience' expresses: in this realm only the individual, with his insights and experiences, can decide. Newman's understanding of conscience is diametrically opposed to this. For him, 'conscience' means man's capacity for truth: the capacity to recognise precisely in the decision-making areas of his life – religion and morals – a truth, the truth. At the same time, conscience – man's capacity to recognise truth – thereby imposes on him the obligation to set out along the path towards truth, to seek it and to submit to it wherever he finds it. Conscience is both capacity for truth and obedience to the truth which manifests itself to anyone who seeks it with an open heart."[178] On his inner journey Newman met many people who gave him important messages for life. But he had to leave most of them behind in order to follow the inner light of his conscience, which for him always represented the most reliable compass. In the *Apologia* he expresses his gratitude to those who accompanied him on a part of the way, also describing how conscience constrained him to make decisions that were not understood and that led him to solitude. But obedience to conscience made him inwardly free from ties of career, honour, and profession, so that he could serve God, the truth, and the Church of Christ. Newman, with the journey of his life, shows us that conscience is not the voice of one's own ego but the echo of God's voice, the advocate of truth in our hearts.

Obedience to the truth led Newman to the haven of the Church of Rome. It has often been emphasised that the *Apologia Pro Vita*

[178] Ibid.

Sua is not an apologia for the Catholic Church, but that Newman simply wanted to shed a light of understanding on the journey of his conscience. In this regard it is true that in the *Apologia* Newman does not so much advance theological as historical arguments. He recounts with extreme sincerity the story of his religious convictions: how, after his first conversion, he became increasingly familiar with the great truths of Christianity; how he strove to reform the Church of England according to the model of the primitive Church and to preserve it from the evil influence of liberalism in religion; how, against his will, he drew ever closer to the Catholic Church and how, finally, after many trials, he came to the conviction that he must take the step of conversion. Newman, in any case, published the *Apologia* with the intent of defending not only himself but also the good name of the Catholic clergy through the public exposition of the story of his religious convictions, with the desire to "tell the truth".[179] For this reason the *Apologia* can also be understood as a defence of the Catholic Church in the form of testimony. Because, as Paul VI said, "modern man listens more willingly to witnesses than to teachers",[180] in our age writings like the *Apologia* are more convincing than purely theoretical arguments. Perhaps we could even say: a true apologia for the Catholic Church in our day must take the form of testimony in order to be credible and convincing. Newman's *Apologia* also contains, in its final chapter, a confession of the infallibility of the Church, which is entrusted with the remedy for humanity's true ills, whose doctrine can protect reason from destructive excesses and which is open to proper scientific research, encouraging and supporting it. The Church urgently needs such witnesses and confessors, who unite faith and reason, thought with life.

179 Newman, *Letters and Diaries*, vol. XXI (Thomas Nelson and Sons Ltd: 1971), p. 103.
180 Paul VI, Apostolic exhortation *Evangelii Nuntiandi*, 8 December 1975, no. 41.

Finally, the *Apologia* also contains a message for the ecumenical movement. It recalls that "there can be no ecumenism worthy of the name without a change of heart."[181] Through sincere conversion many prejudices and misunderstandings can be overcome; various excesses and one-sided views must be removed so that conflicts between theory and practice may not impede progress on the path to unity. For Newman, persevering prayer and lived penance are also essential, while conflicts in doctrine must be addressed starting from Sacred Scripture, the Fathers of the Church, and the great teachers of Christianity. Revealed truth must therefore be obeyed, without compromise or false fears. It has been asked if for the sake of unity it might not have been better for Newman to have remained in the Church of England, working for reunification with the Catholic Church. Newman certainly could have committed himself to the "Catholicisation" of the Church of England, against the will of the bishops. But in doing so he would have renounced his personal integrity, failed to follow his conscience, and also lost his influence. Leaving the Church of England was not easy for Newman; the imperative of conscience, however, was stronger than any purely human consideration. In this command, in fact, Newman recognised the will of God. For him it was clear that the person always has the duty to obey the truth. For this reason too Newman is an eminently ecumenical figure.

181 Vatican Council II, Decree on ecumenism *Unitatis Redintegratio*, no. 7.

V. Aboriginal Vicar of Christ: The Significance of Conscience

Pope Francis wrote in the apostolic exhortation *Amoris Laetitia*: "We have been called to form consciences, not to replace them."[182] It appears obvious that conscience plays a decisive role in the modern person's understanding of himself. In recent decades the magisterium of the Church and experts of moral theology have rightly emphasised the dignity and freedom of conscience, highlighting its irreplaceable role in responsible human action. At the same time they have warned against the danger of subjectivist deviations in which, almost at the opposite extreme of a unilaterally deductive understanding of neo-scholastic stamp, conscience is confused with personal opinion, subjective sentiment, or even arbitrariness.[183]

182 Francis, Post-synodal apostolic exhortation on love in the family *Amoris Laetitia*, 19 March 2016, no. 37.

183 Cf. on the part of the magisterium of the Church: Vatican Council II, Pastoral constitution on the Church in the modern world *Gaudium et Spes*, no. 16; John Paul II, Encyclical letter on some fundamental questions of the Church's moral teaching *Veritatis Splendor*, 6 August 1993, especially nos. 54–64 on "Conscience and truth"; Benedict XVI, Address on the occasion of Christmas greetings to the Roman curia, 20 December 2010; Francis, Post-synodal apostolic exhortation on love in the family *Amoris Laetitia*, 19 March 2016; Francis, Address to the participants in the international conference of moral theology, 13 May 2022. On the part of Catholic moral theology: A. Laun, *Das Gewissen. oberste Norm sittlichen Handelns* (Tyrolia: 1984); E. Schockenhoff, *Das umstrittene Gewissen – Eine theologische Grundlegung* (Matthias-Grünewald-Verlag: 1990); L. Melina, *Morale: tra crisi e rinnovamento. Gli assoluti morali, l'opzione fondamentale, la formazione della coscienza* (Ares: 1993); J. Ratzinger, "Se vuoi la pace, rispetta la coscienza di ogni uomo. Coscienza e verità", in *Cielo e terra. Riflessioni su politica e fede* (Piemme: 1997), pp. 19–49; A. Fumagalli, "Voce di Dio nell'intimo dell'uomo. La coscienza morale secondo S. Agostino", in *La Scuola Cattolica*, 139 (2011), pp. 111–136; H. Schlögel, "Unterschiedliche Akzente

John Henry Newman is sometimes called the 'doctor of conscience'.[184] In his life and thought the subject finds "an attention that had not been seen since Catholic theology perhaps since the time of Augustine".[185] For the English theologian, however, there is no opposition between the primacy of conscience and the primacy of truth. For him conscience does not mean the self-determination of the subject against the demands of truth but the perceptible and imperative presence of the voice of truth within the subject himself.[186] His personal journey constitutes an eloquent testimony to this.

1. Newman, man of conscience

Paul VI, filled with admiration and wonder, said of Newman: "Guided only by love of truth and fidelity to Christ, he traced a path, the most demanding, but also the greatest, the most significant, the most decisive that human thought has ever undertaken during the last century, indeed one might say during modern times, to arrive at the fullness of wisdom and peace."[187] This path was above all a path of obedience to conscience, as two crucial experiences in Newman's life demonstrate in an exemplary way: his first conversion and his move to the Catholic Church.

1.1 The first conversion

Newman grew up in an average Anglican environment in London. Although he read the Bible and cultivated a certain form of religiosity, as a youth he did not have a solid faith in God. When he was fourteen he read authors critical of religion and was tempted to

im lehramtlichen Gewissensverständnis. Das Lehramt seit dem II. Vatikanischen Konzil", in *Internationale Katholische Zeitschrift* 46 (2017), pp. 481–492.

184 Cf. D. Morgan, "John Henry Newman – Doctor of Conscience: Doctor of the Church?", in *Newman Studies Journal* 4 (2007), pp. 5–23.

185 Ratzinger, "Se vuoi la pace, rispetta la coscienza di ogni uomo", p. 32.

186 Cf. ibid., pp. 32f.

187 Paul VI, Address to the pilgrims gathered for the beatification of Dominic of the Mother of God, 27 October 1963.

aim at high ethical ideals but completely abandon his already weak faith in God.

In 1816, in the middle of this inner struggle, he experienced a great change in his mind. His family was then in a precarious situation, and John Henry, ill, had to stay at his boarding school in Ealing. During this period he read Thomas Scott's *The Force of Truth* and was radically shaken: he came to a keen awareness of the reality of God, while at the same time recognising the transience of earthly things. He found peace in the thought of only two absolute beings – the soul and the Creator – beings more real and more important than all the visible things around us.

Newman had found God within himself. In consequence he sought to follow the way of perfection. This effort, however, did not mean a withdrawal into himself but – on the contrary – an opening to the personal God who had spoken to his conscience and shown him his transcendence and closeness. Newman's first conversion consists substantially in the intuition of "a dependence of being on him who is the principle and father of all that is, and particularly on what appears to man as the most inalienable and least contested good: his personal individuality. 'Myself and my Creator' [...] If God is the absolute, all existence finds justification only in a relationship of dependence. And dependence in being demands submission in action."[188]

Newman therefore sought to let himself be guided by that inner voice in which he perceived the echo of the voice of the Invisible: "For indeed I find I have very great need of some monitor to direct me, and I sincerely trust that my conscience, enlightened by the Bible, through the influence of the Holy Spirit, may prove a faithful and vigilant guardian of the true principles of religion."[189] He sincerely followed that "kindly light", even in the difficult

188 J. Honorè, *Itinerario spirituale di Newman* (Morcelliana: 1981), p. 29.
189 Newman, *Autobiographical Writings*, p. 152.

moments of his life,[190] experiencing that "fidelity to conscience leads to an ever deeper conversion".[191]

1.2 The move to the Catholic Church

Newman's conversion to the Catholic Church came after a long and arduous search for truth and a courageous attempt, together with other promoters of the Oxford Movement, to renew the Church of England starting from the ancient Church. In 1841 Newman had written *Tract* 90, seeking to give the Thirty-Nine Articles, the foundation of the Anglican faith, a Catholic interpretation in the spirit of the Church Fathers. The reaction to this attempt was shocking for him: Oxford University condemned the treatise and the bishops of the Church of England rejected his interpretation. Newman then decided to withdraw with some friends to Littlemore, devoting himself entirely to the search for truth.

During his four years at Littlemore Newman followed the principle: "*Do* what your present state of opinion requires in the light of duty, and let that *doing* tell: speak by *acts*."[192] (Emphasis is Newman's.) In 1843 he published a retraction of all his harsh attacks against the Church of Rome and resigned, with deep sorrow, from his office as a minister of the Church of England. The dramatic nature of his quest of conscience emerges plainly from a letter he wrote a few months before his conversion: "The simple question is, Can *I* (it is personal, not whether another, but can *I*) be saved in the English Church? Am *I* in safety, were I to die to-night? Is it a mortal sin in *me*, not joining another communion?"[193] (Emphasis is Newman's.) The question concerning the Church was therefore not secondary

190 Cf. his famous poem "Lead, Kindly Light" (*The Pillar of the Cloud*, 16 June 1833), in J.H. Newman, *Verses on Various Occasions* (Longmans: 1888), p. 156.

191 W.E. Conn, *Conscience & Conversion in Newman: A Developmental Study of Self in John Henry Newman* (Marquette University Press: 2010), p. 25.

192 Newman, *Apologia*, p. 216.

193 Ibid., p. 231.

for Newman. Everything depended on this question: where, today, is the Church founded by Jesus Christ, the Church of the Fathers, the true Church? And this question was connected to another: if *I*, in conscience, am certain that the true Church is that of Rome, can *I* be saved if I do not convert to the Church of Rome? Newman clearly recognised that the question concerning the Church was linked to that of his personal salvation. No other question touches the conscience of the individual in such a radical way.

But Newman still had difficulty with some of Rome's "new" doctrines and practices, and wondered whether they constituted deviations from the pure faith of the ancient Church. He therefore decided to undertake a study of the development of Christian doctrine. When he realised that the "new" doctrines of the Catholic Church were not distortions but developments of the original faith, he set his study aside and decided to convert. Here we see Newman's consistency: what he understood in conscience he immediately put into action. So on 9 October 1845 he embraced the Catholic faith and was received by Blessed Dominic Barberi, an Italian Passionist, into that Church which he had come to know as "the One Fold of Christ".[194]

At the age of 44 Newman left the Church of England and as a result also his friends, his profession, his career. He faithfully followed the call of God, which he had heard in his conscience, and converted to the Church of Rome, in his days a small and despised group of believers at the margins of English society. Conversion to Catholicism was not an easy step for him. On the contrary, it was a matter of obedience to the truth gradually revealed to him in his conscience, even against his own feelings and the bonds of friendship and of long-standing collaboration. Like St Thomas More, Newman followed the call of his conscience, considering it more important than success, public prestige, and the approval

194 Ibid., p. 235.

of prevailing opinion. In him we can admire a true man of conscience: free from personal desires, social expectations, claims to political power, or group consensus, he followed the imperative of truth revealed in his own Christian conscience.[195] Rooted in an intellectual judgement matured over many years, "Newman's ecclesial conversion is best understood as a moral (religious) decision in response to a judgement of personal conscience."[196] All through his life Newman was "one who converted, who was transformed and in this way remained the same, becoming ever more himself".[197]

2. *Newman's thinking on the relationship between conscience, God, and the Church*

Newman's journey of conversion was a journey of conscience, not of self-asserting subjectivity but, quite to the contrary, of obedience to the truth that was gradually opened up to him. Now comes an attempt to summarise, at least in broad outline, Newman's thinking on this topic.[198]

195 Cf. Ratzinger, "Se vuoi la pace, rispetta la coscienza di ogni uomo", pp. 33f.

196 Conn, *Conscience & Conversion in Newman*, p. 95. Cf. Newman's confession in the *Apologia Pro Vita Sua*: "I came to the conclusion that there was no medium, in true philosophy, between Atheism and Catholicity, and that a perfectly consistent mind, under those circumstances in which it finds itself here below, must embrace either the one or the other. And I hold this still: I am a Catholic by virtue of my believing in a God; and if I am asked why I believe in a God, I answer that it is because I believe in myself, for I feel it impossible to believe in my own existence (and of that fact I am quite sure) without believing also in the existence of Him, who lives as a Personal, All-seeing, All-judging Being in my conscience" (p. 198).

197 Benedict XVI, Message on the occasion of the symposium organised by the International Centre of Newman Friends, 18 November 2010.

198 Cf. H. Fries, W. Becker, G. Biemer (eds.), *Newman-Studien, XI: Beiträge zur Gewissensproblematik in historischer, theologischer und pädagogischer Perspektive* (Glock & Lutz: 1980); H. Geissler, *Gewissen und Wahrheit bei John Henry Kardinal Newman* (Peter Lang: 1995); Siebenrock, *Wahrheit, Gewissen und Geschichte*; B. Trocholepczy, "Gewissen: Befähigung und Herausforderung zur conversio continua", in G. Biemer, L. Kuld (eds.), *Newman-Studien*, XVI (Peter Lang: 1998), pp. 51–64; F. Attard, "John Henry Newman. Advocacy of conscience 1825–1832. 1833–1843", in *Salesianum* LXII (2000), pp. 331–351, 433–456; LXIII (2001) 315–340, 521–536; F. Maceri, *La formazione della coscienza del credente. Una proposta educativa alla luce dei Parochial and Plain Sermons di John Henry*

2.1 The significance of conscience

In modern societies the term "conscience" predominantly means the subjectivity of the person, independent of any bond and any form of heteronomy. It is certainly true that everyone must follow their own conscience, just as they must reason with their own reason and feel with their own heart. But Newman vigorously maintains that conscience is not a purely autonomous reality: "Conscience has rights because it has duties; but in this age, with a large portion of the public, it is the very right and freedom of conscience to dispense with conscience, to ignore a Lawgiver and Judge, to be independent of unseen obligations. It becomes a license to take up any or no religion [...]. Conscience is a stern monitor, but in this century it has been superseded by a counterfeit, which the eighteen centuries prior to it never heard of, and could not have mistaken for it, if they had. It is the right of self-will."[199]

Newman highlights that conscience is an essentially theocentric reality – a "sanctuary" in which God personally addresses every individual person, even if they are unaware of it. With Thomas Aquinas Newman affirms that the Creator has imprinted his law in the rational creature. "This law, as apprehended in the minds of individual men, is called 'conscience;' and though it may suffer refraction in passing into the intellectual medium of each, it is not thereby so affected as to lose its character of being the

Newman (Morcelliana: 2001); Association Française des Amis de John Henry Newman, "Le Thème de la conscience dans la pensée de Newman", in *Etudes Newmaniennes* 23 (2007); Morgan, "John Henry Newman – Doctor of Conscience: Doctor of the Church?", pp. 5–23; I. Ker, "Newman, Modernity and Conscience", in E. Botto, H. Geissler (eds.), *Una ragionevole fede. Logos e dialogo in John Henry Newman* (Vita e Pensiero: 2009), pp. 31–38; W.E. Conn, *Conscience & Conversion in Newman: A Developmental Study of Self in John Henry Newman* (Marquette University Press: 2010).

199 J.H. Newman, *A Letter Addressed to His Grace the Duke of Norfolk, on Occasion of Mr. Gladstone's Recent Expostulation* (B.M. Pickering: 1875), p. 58.

Divine Law, but still has, as such, the prerogative of commanding obedience."[200] The human person must obey their conscience, even if it is erroneous, because it presents itself to them as the law of God perceived by their mind. Conscience, therefore, is not simply identical with the law of God; it is the divine law passed through the intellect of the individual person. Here emerges the anthropological dimension of conscience, which, according to Newman, involves not only the capacities of reason[201] but also those of will, feelings, passions, and all the other components of the human person. The formation of conscience therefore concerns the whole person in all their dimensions and is of fundamental importance.

Newman, however, underlines above all the theocentric dimension of conscience, describing it in words that have become famous: "The rule and measure of duty is not utility, nor expedience, nor the happiness of the greatest number, nor State convenience, nor fitness, order, and the *pulchrum*. Conscience is not a long-sighted selfishness, nor a desire to be consistent with oneself; but it is a messenger from Him, who, both in nature and in grace, speaks to us behind a veil, and teaches and rules us by His representatives. Conscience is the aboriginal Vicar of Christ, a prophet in its informations, a monarch in its peremptoriness, a priest in its blessings and anathemas, and, even though the eternal priesthood throughout the Church could cease to be, in it the sacerdotal principle would remain and would have a sway."[202]

In conscience the person does not hear only the voice of their own ego. Newman compares conscience to a messenger of God

200 Ibid., p. 55.

201 The great philosophers and theologians have often distinguished between the perception of moral principles ("synteresis") and their application in concrete circumstances through prudent judgement ("conscience"). Newman does not expand on this anthropological dimension, but presupposes it.

202 Newman, *Letter to the Duke of Norfolk*, p. 57.

who speaks to us as if from behind a veil. This interpretation clearly follows in the footsteps of St Augustine, who often invites the reader to find God and his law in their own heart, and of St Bonaventure, who states: "Conscience is like a herald and messenger of God, and what it says it does not command of itself, but commands as coming from God, like a herald when he proclaims the king's edict. And thus it is that conscience has the power of binding."[203]

Newman even dares to call conscience "the aboriginal vicar of Christ", with a clear reference to the specific mission of the Pope, and to ascribe to it the three "offices" of prophet (in that it tells a person whether a concrete action is good or bad), of king (in that it commands with authority: do this, avoid the other), and of priest (in that it "blesses" after the performance of a good action – a gratifying experience of a good conscience – or "condemns" after a bad action – an expression of a bad conscience). Conscience has an intrinsic openness to Christ. Francesco Maceri therefore concludes that, according to Newman, the formation of conscience "flows into and proceeds along the path of conformation to Christ. It reaches its complete fulfilment in the formation of Christ in us (cf. *Gal* 4:19). [...] Newman situates the summit of the realisation and manifestation of justification and of the enlightened conscience in the welcoming of Christ into the sanctuary of one's heart."[204]

For Newman conscience is "a dutiful obedience to what claims to be a divine voice, speaking within us".[205] For him conscience means a person's capacity to recognise truth in the decisive areas of their existence. At the same time it imposes on them the duty to set out towards the truth, to seek it and to submit to it wherever they encounter it.

203 Bonaventure, *In II librum Sentent.*, dist. 39, a. 1, q. 3, concl.: Ed. Ad Claras Aquas, II, 907b.

204 Maceri, *La formazione della coscienza del credente*, pp. 264f.

205 Newman, *Letter to the Duke of Norfolk*, p. 62.

2.2 Conscience and God

In terms similar to those used by Vatican Council II in no. 16 of the pastoral constitution *Gaudium et Spes,* Newman was convinced that in conscience we can perceive the echo of God's voice. For this reason conscience is for him a way to knowledge of God. In his masterpiece *An Essay in Aid of a Grammar of Assent* (1870) he seeks to develop a "proof" of God starting from the experience of conscience. Analysing the experience of conscience, he distinguishes between the "moral sense" and the "sense of duty".[206] By the moral sense he means the judgement of reason on the goodness or evil of a given action. The sense of duty is instead the authoritative command to carry out the action recognised as good and to avoid that recognised as bad. In his reflections Newman starts above all from this second aspect, considered peculiar to the lived experience of conscience.

Being "imperative and constraining, like no other dictate in the whole of our experience", conscience "has an intimate bearing on our affections and emotions".[207] If we follow the command of conscience we are filled with happiness, joy, and peace. If we do not obey this inner voice we feel shame, dread, and fear. Newman interprets this experience thus: "If, as is the case, we feel responsibility, are ashamed, are frightened, at transgressing the voice of conscience, this implies that there is One to whom we are responsible, before whom we are ashamed, whose claims upon us we fear. If, on doing wrong, we feel the same tearful, broken-hearted sorrow which overwhelms us on hurting a mother; if, on doing right, we enjoy the same sunny serenity of mind, the same soothing, satisfactory delight which follows on our receiving praise from a father,

206 J.H. Newman, *An Essay in Aid of a Grammar of Assent* (Catholic Publication Society: 1870), p. 101.

207 Ibid., p. 103.

we certainly have within us the image of some person, to whom our love and veneration look, in whose smile we find our happiness, for whom we yearn, towards whom we direct our pleadings, in whose anger we are troubled and waste away. [...] And thus the phenomena of Conscience, as a dictate, avail to impress the imagination with the picture of a Supreme Governor, a Judge, holy, just, powerful, all-seeing, retributive."[208]

Newman knows that the experience of conscience does not automatically lead us to God. Only if the voice of conscience is seen in its transcendent character can it become a way to God. In this case it can imprint in us the image of a personal God, as he effectively illustrated in his novel *Callista*. There the protagonist, Callista, states in her dialogue with Polemo: "I feel that God within my heart. I feel myself in His presence. He says to me, 'Do this: don't do that.' You may tell me that this dictate is a mere law of my nature, as to joy or to grieve. I cannot understand this. No, it is the echo of a person speaking to me. Nothing shall persuade me that it does not ultimately proceed from a person external to me. It carries with it its proof of its divine origin. My nature feels towards it as towards a person. When I obey it, I feel a satisfaction; when I disobey, a soreness, – just like that which I feel in pleasing or offending some revered friend. So you see, Polemo, I believe in what is more than a mere 'something.' I believe in what is more real to me than sun, moon, stars, and the fair earth, and the voice of friends. You will say. Who is He? Has He ever told you any thing about Himself? Alas! No! – the more's the pity! But I will not give up what I have, because I have not more. An echo implies a voice; a voice a speaker. That speaker I love and I fear."[209]

Some reproach Newman for having exaggerated the dimension of a person's interiority, even finding in it a way to God. In reality

208 Ibid., pp. 105–106.

209 J.H. Newman, *Callista* (Burns and Lambert: 1855), p. 244.

Newman does not deny the traditional "proofs of God", but he believes that these lead the person to an abstract image of God and do not warm the heart.[210] The way of conscience instead leads the person to a God who is in a personal relationship with everyone, who speaks to them, calls them to conversion, guides them to the knowledge of the truth, spurs them to do good, and presents himself as their supreme Lord.

Newman, however, goes even further, arriving at the conviction that obedience to conscience prepares the person's heart for obedience to faith. In the sermon on "Dispositions for Faith" (1856), he presents some arguments to substantiate this conviction. Again he begins from the experience of conscience as an authoritative voice that demands obedience. Free and mature obedience constitutes precisely that interior attitude which prepares people to open themselves to the Gospel: "[B]eginning with obedience, they go on to the intimate perception and belief of one God. His Voice within them witnesses to Him, and they believe His own witness about Himself. [...] This then is the first step in those good dispositions which lead to faith in the Gospel."[211]

Newman then affirms that the voice of conscience, although imperative, not rarely speaks a silent and imprecise language. It often seems difficult for people to distinguish between the appeals of conscience and the passions of their own hearts. "Thus the gift of conscience creates a desire for what it does not fully supply. It awakens in them the idea of an authoritative guide, of a divine law; and the desire to possess it in its fullness and not merely in fragments or indirect suggestions. It creates in them a thirst, a longing to know that invisible Lord, that Sovereign, that Judge, who now speaks to them only secretly, whispers to their hearts, tells them

210 Cf. id., *Apologia*, pp. 241f.

211 J.H. Newman, *Sermons Preached on Various Occasions* (Burns and Lambert: 1857), pp. 74–75.

something, but certainly not all, that they desire and need. [...] Such is the definition, I may say, of every religious man, who has not the knowledge of Christ: he is on the look-out."[212] The commands of conscience therefore arouse in people the desire for a clearer and more certain orientation, and even for a Saviour who can free us from sin and give us peace.

Drawing from his experience, Newman can testify that "obedience to conscience leads to obedience to the Gospel, which, instead of being something different altogether, is but the completion and perfection of that religion which natural conscience teaches."[213] Obedience to conscience prepares the human heart for faith, which for its part purifies and enlightens the conscience. In Sacred Scripture, Newman wrote, the person "will find all those vague conjectures and imperfect notions about Truth, which his own heart taught him, abundantly sanctioned, completed, and illustrated".[214] By docilely welcoming the Gospel, the human conscience becomes a Christian conscience, that is, informed and purified by faith. Revealed truth, in fact, enlightens the conscience in such a way that in the concrete circumstances of life it can more easily make sound judgements according to the demands of the Gospel. Even more: in Christ, through baptism, the whole person, and therefore also their conscience, is born again.[215]

3. Conscience and Church

Newman's most significant insights on the theme of conscience and Church are found in the aforementioned *Letter to the Duke of Norfolk*. In this essay Newman rejects Mr Gladstone's accusation that after the proclamation of the dogma of papal infallibility

212 Ibid., pp. 75–76.

213 J.H. Newman, *Parochial and Plain Sermons*, vol. VIII (Rivingtons: 1868), p. 202.

214 Ibid., vol. I, p. 217.

215 Cf. id., *Apologia*, p. 248.

Catholics could no longer serve the state as good citizens, since they would be obliged to surrender their conscience to the Pope. To respond to such ideas Newman seeks to clarify the relationship between the authority of conscience and that of the Pope.[216]

The Pope's authority is grounded in Revelation, which expresses the divine goodness towards humanity. God has given his Revelation to the Church, and by the power of his Spirit he ensures that it is faithfully preserved, interpreted, and transmitted in the Church and through the Church. If a person accepts in faith this mission of the Church, he understands in his own conscience that he is obliged to obey the Church, especially its supreme pastor. Newman, consequently, can write: "Did the Pope speak against Conscience in the true sense of the word, he would commit a suicidal act. He would be cutting the ground from under his feet. [...] On the law of conscience and its sacredness are founded both his authority in theory and his power in fact. [...] The championship of the Moral Law and of conscience is his *raison d'être.*"[217] Catholics obey the Pope not because they are forced to do so but because they have the conviction, in faith, that – through him and the bishops in communion with him – the Lord continues to guide the Church, preserving it in truth and communion.

A formed conscience leads the believer to free and mature obedience towards the Pope. Conversely, the Church, the Pope, and the bishops enlighten the conscience, which needs clear and precise support: "The sense of right and wrong, which is the first element in religion, is so delicate, so fitful, so easily puzzled, obscured, perverted, so subtle in its argumentative methods, so impressible by education, so biassed by pride and passion, so unsteady in its flight,

216 Cf. J. Honoré, "Autorité dans l' Eglise et liberté de conscience", in Strolz, Binder (eds.), *Lover of Truth*, pp. 61–78; I. Ker, "Newman, Modernity and Conscience", in E. Botto, H. Geissler (eds.), *Una ragionevole fede. Logos e dialogo in John Henry Newman* (Vita e Pensiero: 2009), pp. 30–38.

217 Newman, *Letter to the Duke of Norfolk*, p. 60.

that, in the struggle for existence amid various exercises and triumphs of the human intellect, this sense is at once the highest of all teachers, yet the least luminous; and the Church, the Pope, the Hierarchy are, in the Divine purpose, the supply of an urgent demand."[218] Conscience is "the first element" in religion in that it constitutes a ray of God's truth in the heart of every person. But this ray of truth, exposed to many winds, is often obscured, confused, or perverted, and urgently needs external help. Newman convincingly explains that the Church has "a maieutic function": it "imposes nothing foreign, but brings to fruition what is proper to anamnesis, namely its interior openness to the truth".[219]

Conscience, therefore, maintains its primacy, and "it is never lawful to go against our conscience."[220] This statement, however, must be correctly understood: while it is never a sin to follow one's conscience – indeed one must – it can be a sin to have arrived at erroneous and distorted convictions due to a lack of willingness to form one's conscience. The Church offers great assistance in this formation of the conscience of the individual believer, as well as that of society, being the advocate and witness of truth and also of the inalienable duties, rights, and freedoms of humanity. These duties, rights, and freedoms, rooted in the dignity of the human person, form the basis of modern constitutional states, but as such they cannot be subjected to majoritarian democratic rules. In defending the dignity of the human person, created by God and redeemed by Christ, and in reaffirming his or her fundamental rights and duties, the Church therefore carries out a mission of extraordinary importance for modern societies.

The authority of the Church and the Pope therefore serves the conscience of the believer and of society. This authority, however,

218 Ibid., pp. 60–61.

219 Ratzinger, *Benedict XVI and Cardinal Newman* (Family Publications: 2005) p. 50.

220 Newman, *Letter to the Duke of Norfolk*, p. 56.

also has limits. It has nothing in common with arbitrariness or the models of domination of this world, being inseparably connected to the sense of faith of all the people of God and the specific mission of theologians. The infallible authority of the Church concerns the realm of revealed truth and that which is necessary for salvation. If the Pope makes decisions in the fields of discipline or administration, these are obviously not infallible statements. This applies all the more if the Pope offers commentary on current issues, for example, in the field of politics.

In our day some have cited Newman to justify conscientious dissent from the magisterium of the Church and the Pope. Newman, however, expressly states that "conscience is not a judgement upon any speculative truth, any abstract doctrine, but bears immediately on conduct, on something to be done or not done. [...] Hence conscience cannot come into direct collision with the Church's or the Pope's infallibility; which is engaged only on general propositions, or the condemnation of propositions simply particular."[221] Newman would certainly have rejected the idea that on the basis of one's conscience a Catholic could dissent from the Church's doctrine on faith or morals. Only if one loses one's faith, or maintains, because of an erroneous conscience, that another religion is the true one, is one required to leave the Church, as has always been taught by the great teachers.[222]

221 Ibid., p. 62.

222 Cf. Ker, *Newman, Modernity and Conscience*, p. 34. According to Ian Ker, Newman would have been alarmed by the possible conscientious dissent of a faithful Catholic towards the Church's moral doctrine, but also by the idea that the role of conscience in moral norms could be ignored. As for positive moral norms, it seems obvious that it is up to the individual's conscience to concretise them and put them into practice according to his own capabilities. As for negative moral norms, one might ask whether there is room for the action of conscience in these respects, given that these are always obligatory, without any exception. According to Ker, Newman would argue that conscience also plays a fundamental role with regard to negative moral norms, because they must be understood correctly, grasped in their precise meaning, and respected faithfully in the concrete situations of life.

Newman adds, "Conscience being a practical dictate, a collision is possible between it and the Pope's authority only when the Pope legislates, or gives particular orders, and the like. But a Pope is not infallible in his laws, nor in his commands, nor in his acts of state, nor in his administration, nor in his public policy."[223] Also in these areas the Catholic, according to Newman, will readily accept the Pope's decisions so as not to endanger the unity of the Church. In individual cases, however, one may in conscience arrive at a position different from that of the Pope.

Even so, in this regard Newman offers clear criteria for the believer: "*Prima facie* it is his bounden duty, even from a sentiment of loyalty, to believe the Pope right and to act accordingly. He must vanquish that mean, ungenerous, selfish, vulgar spirit of his nature, which, at the very first rumour of a command, places itself in opposition to the Superior who gives it, asks itself whether he is not exceeding his right, and rejoices, in a moral and practical matter, to commence with scepticism. He must have no wilful determination to exercise a right of thinking, saying, doing just what he pleases, the question of truth and falsehood, right and wrong, the duty if possible of obedience, the love of speaking as his Head speaks, and of standing in all cases on his Head's side, being simply discarded. If this necessary rule were observed, collisions between the Pope's authority and the authority of conscience would be very rare. On the other hand, in the fact that, after all, in extraordinary cases, the conscience of each individual is free, we have a safeguard and security [...] that no Pope ever will be able [...] to create a false conscience for his own ends."[224] The Pope is not above the truth; he is the vicar of Christ, and therefore also the servant of the truth that enlightens the conscience of the faithful.

According to Newman, a Catholic is called to accept the Church's teaching and put it into practice in the joys and struggles of each day.

223 Newman, *Letter to the Duke of Norfolk*, p. 62.

224 Ibid., p. 64.

It is also necessary to accept the Pope's laws and orders, taking into account the aforementioned guidelines that help one be as in tune with the Pope as possible, without ruling it out that in extraordinary cases the conscience might come to a different judgement.

Newman concludes these reflections on conscience with a famous toast: "If I am obliged to bring religion into after-dinner toasts, (which indeed does not seem quite the thing) I shall drink, – to the Pope, if you please, – still, to Conscience first, and to the Pope afterwards."[225] This quip, which also expresses Newman's fine sense of humour, means first of all that our obedience to the Pope is not blind obedience, but supported by a conscience shaped by faith. Then again, the Pope's authority is not absolute and does not replace the authority of conscience. In this sense conscience truly comes first, as the inner capacity for truth, and then the Pope, the representative of authority at the service of truth.

Newman firmly maintains the correlation between conscience and Church. It is not possible to appeal to him or his words to create oppositions between the authority of conscience and that of the Pope (or the Church). Both authorities, the subjective and the objective, remain dependent on each other: the Pope on conscience and conscience on the Pope, because both serve the truth, which – in the final analysis – is the Lord Jesus himself (cf. *John* 14:6).

With his life's journey and his solid doctrine John Henry Newman can help us rediscover the true significance of conscience as an echo of God's voice, while rejecting insufficient and reductive interpretations. Newman always fully affirmed the dignity and primacy of conscience, never deviating from the path of objective truth. For him conscience is the advocate of truth in our hearts, it is "the aboriginal Vicar of Christ".

225 Ibid., p. 66.

VI. *Cor ad Cor Loquitur*: The Inner Dispositions of the Apostle

At the beatification of John Henry Newman in Birmingham on 19 September 2010, Benedict XVI preached on the importance of this great theologian for our time. He commended him first of all for "his insights into the relationship between faith and reason, into the vital place of revealed religion in civilised society, and into the need for a broadly-based and wide-ranging approach to education" – insights that not only were profoundly significant for his time but continue to inspire and enlighten many people all over the world. On this particular occasion, however, Benedict XVI then preferred to reflect above all on "his life as a priest, a pastor of souls", on "the warmth and humanity underlying his appreciation of the pastoral ministry", on "his devoted care for the people of Birmingham during the years that he spent at the Oratory he founded, visiting the sick and the poor, comforting the bereaved, caring for those in prison".[226]

Continuing in the train of these thoughts Pope Francis, on the occasion of Newman's canonisation in St Peter's Square on 13 October 2019, highlighted "the holiness of daily life, which St John Henry Newman described in these words: 'The Christian has a deep, silent, hidden peace, which the world sees not.... The Christian is cheerful, easy, kind, gentle, courteous, candid, unassuming; has no pretense ... with so little that is unusual or striking

226 Benedict XVI, Homily at the Mass of beatification of Cardinal John Henry Newman, 19 September 2010.

in his bearing, that he may easily be taken at first sight for an ordinary man.' Let us ask to be like that, 'kindly lights' amid the encircling gloom. Jesus, 'stay with me, and then I shall begin to shine as Thou shinest: so to shine as to be a light to others.'"[227]

In both his Anglican and his Catholic period Newman's life and pastoral commitment were profoundly marked by his fatherly love for souls. The words he chose for his motto as cardinal – *Cor ad cor loquitur* – express well this fundamental attitude of his. His thoughts, teachings, and writings were not simply academic in character, but always also an expression of his zeal for souls.

So it is not surprising that Newman had a special interior relationship with St Paul, the great missionary of the primitive Church and spiritual father of many Christian communities. According to him, Paul was "this glorious Apostle, this sweetest of inspired writers, this most touching and winning of teachers", for whom he had "ever felt a special devotion".[228] Newman left us four sermons devoted entirely to the apostle to the Gentiles. The theme of these spiritual lectures is not so much Paul's apostolic activity as the sentiments and inner attitude that characterise his work of evangelisation. Newman's reflections have lost none of their freshness and can help Christians, at the beginning of the 21st century, to rediscover and deepen their missionary vocation, according to Cardinal Newman's motto: *Cor ad cor loquitur.*

1. A heart transformed by grace

No one can be an apostle unless he has been seized and transformed by the grace of God. In an early sermon that dates back to the period when he was still an Anglican, Newman speaks of the

227 Francis, Homily at the Mass and canonisation of the Blesseds John Henry Newman, Giuseppina Vannini, Mariam Thresia Chiramel Mankidiyan, Dulce Lopes Pontes, Marguerite Bays, 13 October 2019.

228 Newman, *Sermons Preached on Various Occasions*, p. 104.

conversion of St Paul in relation to his ministry.[229] For Newman Saul's experience of conversion is the actual beginning of Paul's ministry. What does he mean by this?

Saul – Newman says – is known as the chief persecutor of Christians: he approves the stoning of Stephen, who, dying, prays for his killers; afterward he obtains permission from the religious leaders to imprison the disciples of the new Way who are in Damascus, but before the gates of the city he is "struck down by a miracle, and converted to the faith he persecuted".[230] Paul's conversion is first of all a demonstration of God's power, of his triumph over the Enemy: "To show His power, He put forth His hand into the very midst of the persecutors of His Son, and seized upon the most strenuous among them."[231] At the same time this conversion is the fruit of Stephen's fervent prayer: "The prayers of righteous men avail much. The first Martyr had power with God to raise up the greatest Apostle."[232] No one can be an apostle if they do not trust in the transforming power of God and in the power of intercessory prayer.

The grace of conversion, a mystery of God's providence, makes Paul a shining example of an apostle. In his life he experiences both the limitations of sin and the power of God's mercy, which captivates him to the point of making him a spiritual father to the Gentiles: "In the history of his sin and its most gracious forgiveness, he exemplifies far more than his brother Apostles his own Gospel; that we are all guilty before God, and can be saved only by His free bounty."[233] Like Paul, every apostle is called to witness to God's mercy, first with their life and then with their words.

229 J.H. Newman, *Parochial and Plain Sermons*, vol. II, pp. 95–106.

230 Ibid., p. 96.

231 Ibid., p. 97.

232 Ibid., p. 96.

233 Ibid., p. 99.

The life Paul had led before his conversion makes him particularly suited to be an instrument for carrying out God's plan for the Gentiles. Of course, caution is needed, because the spread of the Gospel is not in the first place the work of humanity but of divine grace. God, however, almost always uses human help to carry out his plans. Paul is as if predestined for the mission to the pagans – not only because of his knowledge and spiritual gifts but also and above all because of his journey of faith and conversion. This journey teaches him not to be discouraged by the gravity of the sin committed, to be able to find the sparks of faith hidden in people, to identify with the most diverse types of temptation, to bear with humility the grandeur of the revelations received, and to use his own experiences wisely for the conversion of others. Thus Paul becomes "the comforter, help, and guide of his brethren", because he was given "to know in some good measure the *hearts of men*".[234] (Emphasis is Newman's.) It is comforting to know that all life experiences – positive and negative – can be useful in spreading the Gospel according to God's plan.

Of course, with these thoughts Newman does not mean that one must first sin in order to become an apostle and a saint. Paul did not become a better Christian because of his sin, but it "rendered him *more fitted for a particular purpose* in God's providence, – more fitted, when converted, to reclaim others".[235] (Emphasis is Newman's.) Newman clearly states that Paul's life before his conversion was not an impious or immoral life: he listened to the voice of his conscience and did not proudly turn against God. But the voice of Paul's conscience was not sufficiently enlightened by Sacred Scripture, as it was, for example, for Simeon and Anna, who on the basis of the Old Testament had recognised Jesus as

234 Ibid., p. 101.

235 Ibid., p. 102.

the awaited Saviour. Paul instead had not recognised Christ and became a persecutor of Christians.

What consequences for the individual Christian does Newman draw from these reflections? Every believer must "cherish and obey the holy light of conscience within him, as Saul did; let him carefully study the Scriptures, as Saul did not; and the God who had mercy even on the persecutor of His saints, will assuredly shed His grace upon him, and bring him into the truth as it is in Jesus."[236] The believer who wants to become an apostle listens to the voice of conscience and the word of Revelation, makes them their examiners, lets themself be transformed, and is attentive to welcoming God's ever-new call.

2. *A heart for human nature*

The profound union with Christ that results from every authentic conversion leads St Paul to say: "It is no longer I who live, but Christ who lives in me; and the life I now live in the flesh I live by faith in the Son of God, who loved me and gave himself for me" (*Gal* 2:20). Some saints are so filled with the life of God that they lose themselves entirely in it and apparently have nothing left of human nature. As Newman shows in his sermon "St Paul's Characteristic Gift",[237] the apostle to the Gentiles belongs to that other group of saints "in whom the supernatural combines with nature, instead of superseding it, – invigorating it, elevating it, ennobling it; and who are not the less men, because they are saints".[238] In this sermon, which Newman delivered at the university church in Dublin a few years after his conversion to the Catholic Church, he asks what is the characteristic mark that distinguishes Paul from the other saints. According to him, the apostle to the Gentiles is characterised above

236 Ibid., p. 106.

237 Newman, *Sermons Preached on Various Occasions*, p. 109.

238 Ibid., p. 105.

all by the fact that the fullness of divine gifts does not destroy what is human in him, but elevates and perfects it.

As a result Paul understands human nature particularly well, with all its strengths and weaknesses, temptations, aspirations and inclinations: "Human nature, the common nature of the whole race of Adam, spoke in him, acted in him, with an energetical presence, with a sort of bodily fulness, always under the sovereign command of divine grace, but losing none of its real freedom and power because of its subordination. And the consequence is, that, having the nature of man so strong within him, he is able to enter into human nature, and to sympathise with it, with a gift peculiarly his own."[239]

The apostle, despite having lived a life of rigour before his conversion, now numbers himself among the despised pagans and speaks as if he were one of them. He feels that he shares the lot of his fellow men, of the entire lineage of Adam. So he is aware of possessing a nature compromised by the whole gamut of emotions, inclinations, intentions, and sins that characterise a person's life in the world; it is in this sense that Paul, in the footsteps of the Lord, bears upon himself the sin of all people and feels in full communion with them. "He, I say, a strict Pharisee, (as he describes himself), blameless according to legal justice, conversing with all good conscience before God, serving God from his forefathers with a pure conscience, he nevertheless elsewhere speaks of himself as a profligate heathen outcast, before the grace of God called him."[240] Paul does not point the finger at others, because he is aware that sin and concupiscence are present in him too. He is a great expert on human nature "because he vividly apprehended, in that nature of his which grace has sanctified, what it was in its tendencies and results when deprived of grace".[241] The missionary disciple

239 Ibid., p. 109.
240 Ibid., p. 110.
241 Ibid., p. 111.

is always on the path of conversion and renewal in Christ. He is able to identify with and share the different life situations of men, to experience the same emotions, to understand their struggles, to take part in their joys and concerns.

Paul also shows his love for human nature by not hesitating to resort to pagan authors. Newman refers to three well-known passages in which the apostle quotes Greek writers: in the Areopagus of Athens, when he refers to the inscription on an altar that says: "to an unknown god" (*Acts* 17:23). Then, when he reminds the Corinthians of a maxim of the poet Menander: "Bad company ruins good morals" (*1 Cor* 15:33). And finally in the Letter to Titus, in which he quotes the philosopher Epimenides: "Cretans are always liars, evil beasts, lazy gluttons" (*Titus* 1:12). Why does Paul quote pagan authors? Newman answers: "He was a true lover of souls. He loved poor human nature with a passionate love, and the literature of the Greeks was only its expression; and he hung over it tenderly and mournfully, wishing for its regeneration and salvation."[242] God's plan of salvation also includes the Greeks – it includes all peoples. While Paul clearly teaches "that the heathens are in darkness, and in sin, and under the power of the Evil One, he will not allow that they are beyond the eye of Divine Mercy".[243] The apostle never rejects what is truly human. He has a great and welcoming heart because he is convinced that God wills the salvation of all.

Finally, Paul emphasises that all people are children of Adam, and "had pleasure in thinking that all men were brethren".[244] He does not limit himself to emphasising that all humanity descends from Adam, but also "tenderly contemplates the captivity, and the anguish, and the longing, and the deliverance of poor human

242 Ibid., p. 112.

243 Ibid.

244 Ibid., p. 113.

nature".[245] According to the Letter to the Romans, "the creation waits with eager longing for the revealing of the sons of God" (*Rom* 8:19). The apostle gives constant reminders that all people have the same origin and the same end: they come from God and are called to a life of glory in God.

3. A heart for his people

Newman does not fail to speak also of Paul's love for Israel, his people. If the apostle feels connected to the whole human race, "if he felt so much for all races spread over the earth, what did he feel for his own nation! O what a special mixture, bitter and sweet, of generous pride (if I may so speak), but of piercing, overwhelming anguish, did the thought of the race of Israel inflict upon him!"[246]

Even after his conversion Paul continues to take pride in God's election of his people. This is particularly evident in his Letter to the Romans, where he writes: "They are Israelites, and to them belong the sonship, the glory, the covenants, the giving of the law, the worship, and the promises; to them belong the patriarchs, and of their race, according to the flesh, is the Christ, who is God over all, blessed for ever. Amen" (*Rom* 9:4–5). With what gratitude does Paul look to Israel, "the highest of nations and the lowest, his own dear people, whose glories were before his imagination and in his affection from his childhood".[247]

This sentiment of pride and gratitude, however, is accompanied by sadness and pain (cf. *Rom* 9:2). In fact, the very people who for centuries had awaited the Messiah, who prepared the way and announced his coming, did not receive him. Paul could well understand the obstinacy of the Israelites, since he too, before his conversion, had cultivated the same feelings and thoughts about

245 Ibid.

246 Ibid., p. 114.

247 Ibid.

Jesus. Out of compassion he interceded, like Moses, for his people; indeed, out of love for his brothers and sisters he exclaimed that he wished "that I myself were accursed and cut off from Christ" (*Rom* 9:3). He was ready to give everything for the love of his people. "He pleaded for them, while they were persecuting his Lord and himself. He reminded his Lord that he himself had also been that Lord's persecutor."[248] His heart bleeds because of Israel's hardness of heart, so as to make him exclaim: "O dearest ones, O glorious race, O miserably fallen!"[249]

At the same time – despite everything – Paul does not lose hope for his people. After admitting that most Israelites had rejected Jesus, he consoled himself with the idea that their obstinacy would become a blessing for the Gentiles, and he was full of confidence in the prophecy of "their recovery in time to come",[250] through which they too would subsequently be saved. So he writes in his Letter to the Romans: "A hardening has come upon part of Israel, until the full number of the Gentiles come in, and so all Israel will be saved" (*Rom* 11:25–26).

Every Christian who has become an apostle will feel the same sentiments concerning their family and their people: full of gratitude for all the good and beauty they have received, in a sincere readiness to intercede for those who do not know or have forgotten the Lord, with unshakeable trust in God's mercy for all.

4. *A heart for believers*

In a sermon Newman delivered shortly thereafter, again at the university church in Dublin, he portrays the apostle's love for Christians. The title of this homily is "St Paul's Gift of Sympathy".[251] Newman

248 Ibid., p. 115.

249 Ibid., p. 114.

250 Ibid., p. 117.

251 Newman, *Sermons Preached on Various Occasions*, pp. 121–138.

continues the reasoning begun in the previous sermon and shows the affection with which the apostle treats his brothers and sisters in the faith. He highlights his *humanitas*: "a virtue which comes of His supernatural grace, and is cultivated for His sake, though its object is human nature, viewed in itself, in its intellect, its affections, and its history. And it is this virtue which I consider is so characteristic of St Paul; and he himself often inculcates it in his Epistles, as when he enjoins bowels of mercy, benignity, kindness, gentleness, and the like."[252] How is this attitude evident in the apostle's life and work?

Newman emphasises that Paul is so full of love for others that "in the tenor of his daily thoughts, he almost loses sight of his gifts and privileges, his station and dignity, except he is called by duty to remember them, and he is to himself merely a frail man speaking to frail men, and he is tender towards the weak from a sense of his own weakness."[253] Paul knows that not only do others need God's mercy, but he himself does first. In fact, he prefers to call himself a servant: "For what we preach is not ourselves, but Jesus Christ as Lord, with ourselves as your servants for Jesus' sake" (*2 Cor* 4:5). And he confesses his own weakness: "But we have this treasure in earthen vessels, to show that the transcendent power belongs to God and not to us" (*2 Cor* 4:7). The apostle is aware of his own misery; he knows that he depends on the grace of God. It is precisely this awareness that unites him even more closely with his spiritual children.

In his speeches and letters Paul continually speaks of his weakness: "For even when we came into Macedonia, our bodies had no rest but we were afflicted at every turn – fighting without and fear within" (*2 Cor* 7:5). Describing his apostolate in Corinth, he states: "I was with you in weakness and in much fear and trembling; and

252 Ibid., pp. 124–125.
253 Ibid., p. 125.

my speech and my message were not in plausible words of wisdom, but in demonstration of the Spirit and of power" (*1 Cor* 2:3–4). Speaking of the revelations that the Lord gave him, he does not fail to recall that "a thorn was given me in the flesh, a messenger of Satan, to harass me, to keep me from being too elated" (*2 Cor* 12:7). Nor does he leave out his harsh interior struggles: "For we do not want you to be ignorant, brethren, of the affliction we experienced in Asia; for we were so utterly, unbearably crushed that we despaired of life itself" (*2 Cor* 1:8). When he bids farewell to the elders of Miletus, he says: "You yourselves know how I lived among you all the time from the first day that I set foot in Asia, serving the Lord with all humility and with tears and with trials" (*Acts* 20:18–19). Why does Paul speak so frankly and naturally about his weaknesses and inner struggles? Newman explains: a man who knows how to strip himself of his greatness and put himself on his brothers' level shows a profound sharing in human nature; a man who speaks with simplicity and communicates his emotions is able to feel and manifest a great love for all and at the same time make himself loved.[254] Being an apostle should not be confused with worldly heroism or human perfectionism. To fulfil his plan of salvation God needs not perfect hearts but hearts filled with love: hearts engulfed in his fire, hearts that are purified and transformed by it, hearts that with their inner light attract others and with love lead them to Christ.

Newman repeatedly reiterates that the grace in Paul's heart does not repress human nature, but sanctifies and ennobles it. He retains all the human, but not the sinful, that was in him. He lives in communion with his beloved Lord and at the same time is always sensitive to people's feelings and to the world around him. Newman sees in this the essence of the humanity of Paul's heart: "Wonderful to say, he who had rest and peace in the love of Christ, was not

[254] Cf. ibid.

satisfied without the love of man; he whose supreme reward was the approbation of God, looked out for the approval of his brethren. He who depended solely on the Creator, yet made himself dependent on the creature. Though he had that which was Infinite, he would not dispense with the finite. He loved his brethren, not only 'for Jesus's sake', to use his own expression, but for their own sake also. He lived in them; he felt with them and for them; he was anxious about them; he gave them help, and in turn he looked for comfort from them. His mind was like some instrument of music, harp or viol, the strings of which vibrate, though untouched, by the notes which other instruments give forth, and he was ever, according to his own precept, 'rejoicing with them that rejoice, and weeping with them that weep'; and thus he was the least magisterial of all teachers, and the gentlest and most amiable of all rulers."[255]

Particularly strong is Paul's bond with his friends and colleagues, in every circumstance of life. He rejoices "at the coming of Stephanas and Fortunatus and Achaicus" (*1 Cor* 16:17). He writes: "My mind could not rest because I did not find my brother Titus there" (*2 Cor* 2:13). And then: "But God, who comforts the downcast, comforted us by the coming of Titus" (*2 Cor* 7:6). Of the Church of Rome, he greets Phoebe, Prisca and Aquila, and "the church in their house", Epaenetus, Mary, Andronicus, and Junias, and many other brothers and sisters (cf. *Rom* 16). He tells us that Epaphroditus was "near to death. But God had mercy on him, and not only on him but on me also, lest I should have sorrow upon sorrow" (*Phil* 2:27). He complains that "all who are in Asia turned away from me" (*2 Tim* 1:15), and in another passage: "At my first defense no one took my part; all deserted me. May it not be charged against them!" (*2 Tim* 4:16). Some of his friends distanced themselves from him: "Demas, in love with this present world,

[255] Ibid., pp. 130–131.

has deserted me […]. Luke alone is with me" (*2 Tim* 4:10–11). At the end of the Second Letter to Timothy he writes: "Greet Prisca and Aquila, and the household of Onesiphorus. Erastus remained at Corinth; Trophimus I left ill at Miletus. Do your best to come before winter. Eubulus sends greetings to you, as do Pudens and Linus and Claudia and all the brethren" (*2 Tim* 4:19–21). What greatness of brotherly love, what trust, what sensitivity and also what compassion and sorrow these words express! Newman is deeply touched by this, and writes: "He, in a word, who is the special preacher of Divine Grace, is also the special friend and intimate of human nature. He who reveals to us the mystery of God's Sovereign Decrees, manifests at the same time the tenderest interest in the souls of individuals."[256] The true Christian has a big heart; they think of the whole world and pray for all. But at the same time they turn to each with love and fellowship, because they are aware of the singular dignity and vocation of each and because they have at heart the salvation of every single person.

This love of Paul for all people explains well the apostle's indignation over the feelings of jealousy, envy, and rivalry in the Christian communities. He considers these attitudes shameful and irreverent not only towards Christ but also towards the common human nature that gives to all the same dignity and the same right to the title of men or women.[257] Paul loved humanity so much that "he sympathised with them all, wherever and whatever they were; and he felt it to be one special mercy, conveyed to them in the Gospel, that the unity of human nature was henceforth recognised and restored in Jesus Christ. The spirit of party, then, was simply antagonistic to the spirit of the Apostle, and a great offence to him, even when it did not go so far as schism."[258] Of the community

256 Ibid., p. 133.
257 Cf. ibid.
258 Ibid., pp. 133–134.

of Corinth, divided because some recognised Paul as their teacher, others Apollos, still others Cephas, and still others Christ, he asked: "Is Christ divided?" (*1 Cor* 1:13). Among those regenerated by grace "there cannot be Greek and Jew, circumcised and uncircumcised, barbarian, Scythian, slave, free man, but Christ is all, and in all" (*Col* 3:11). The believer with an apostolic heart, in the depths of his heart, nourishes the same profound aspiration as Jesus and repeats with him the prayer: *May they all be one.* They are a servant of unity in Christ and know that Christian witness can be credible only on this condition: "that they may all be one [...] so that the world may believe" (*John* 17:21).

5. A heart that trusts in the Lord

Some brief notes have also come down to us from another sermon by Newman as a Catholic, on the theme of "St Paul the Type of the Church as Missionarising".[259] The fundamental thoughts of this sermon, not written out but delivered off the cuff, complete our meditation on the apostle's inner dispositions.

Newman begins this homily with the statement that Paul was above all a sower of the word: "He sowed in all places." And he was also a champion – not only like David against Goliath – but "against the world".[260] This action, begun by Paul, is continued by the Church in every place and time. And not only that of sowing but also that of the good fight of faith.

Paul is the model of this par excellence: he fought in faith against the zealots of Judaism – one need think only of the forty men who "bound themselves by an oath neither to eat nor drink till they had killed Paul" (*Acts* 23:12); he also had to fight against fanatics of paganism, as shown, for example, by the riot of the

259 J.H. Newman, "On St Paul the Type of the Church as Missionarising" (23 February 1851), in id., *Sermon Notes of John Henry Cardinal Newman, 1849–1878* (Longmans, Green: 1913), pp. 62–64.

260 Ibid., p. 62.

silversmiths of Ephesus (cf. *Acts* 19:21ff.). He had to confront the indifferent, for example, the governor Festus, who declared him mad (cf. *Acts* 26:24), or the Greek philosophers in the Areopagus, who, after his speech on the resurrection, mocked him and told him they would hear him another time (cf. *Acts* 17:32).

Newman applies these examples to his own time: the Church in 19th-century England had to fight against evangelical fanaticism and the indifference of statesmen. The former labelled Rome the Antichrist; the latter cared only for their own political gain. This certainly applies to our time as well: hostility on one side and indifference on the other make it difficult for many to accept the message of the Gospel and bear witness to it.

Newman, however, is in no way pessimistic; on the contrary, he is full of confidence, because he sees in faith the greatness and unity of the Church of all times: "This awful unity of the Church is our consolation." It shows that "the Church comes from God" and "nothing comes strange and new to her".[261] This leads him to conclude that this is the essential and permanent vocation of all members of the Church: "our business to sow and to fight, and to leave the rest to God".[262]

Conclusion

It is striking that Newman, in his homilies on St Paul, does not describe any grand missionary strategy or highlight the apostle's impressive activities. For him it seems to be not so much his outward action that is decisive but the movements of his heart, from which, as from a gushing spring, every thought, word, and action flows. It could be said that in these sermons Newman wants to outline the inner profile of the true apostle. The tiles of the mosaic that distinguish the portrait of the authentic apostle are: readiness

261 Ibid., pp. 63–64.
262 Ibid., p. 64.

for conversion, which with God's grace becomes a personal experience that makes one's life a model for others as well; knowledge of human nature, which is a great help in understanding others deeply, in being in harmony with them, in sharing their joys and concerns; love for one's people, which is shown in gratitude, the desire to intercede, and hope for all; communion with one's brothers and sisters in faith that leads one to become all things to all; the courage to engage in the good fight of faith, without which it is impossible in this world to lead others to the Gospel; but above all, unshakable trust in the power of Jesus's love. The main task of the Christian, in fact, is to sow the seed of the Word generously and let God determine when and how it will bear fruit.

Pope Leo XIV reiterated in his very first greeting to the faithful that he wanted to serve "with you as a Church, united" in order "to act as men and women faithful to Jesus Christ, in order to proclaim the Gospel without fear, to be missionaries".[263] Starting from St Paul, Newman shows us what it means to have a missionary heart: such a heart is touched by the heart of the Saviour; it addresses itself personally and with love – *cor ad cor* – to brothers and sisters in faith, but also to those who do not believe or are seeking the meaning of life; it trusts unshakably in the love of the Lord, who promised: "And I, when I am lifted up from the earth, will draw all men to myself" (*John* 12:32).

263 Pope Leo XIV, First blessing "Urbi et Orbi", 8 May 2025.